Robert Lowell's Life and Work

POETS ON POETRY · Donald Hall, General Editor

Richard Tillinghast

Robert Lowell's
Life and Work
DAMAGED GRANDEUR

Ann Arbor

THE UNIVERSITY OF MICHIGAN PRESS

1998   1997   1996   1995   4   3   2   1

A CIP catalogue record for this book is available from the British Library.

Library of Congress Cataloging-in-Publication Data

Tillinghast, Richard.
    Robert Lowell's life and work : damaged grandeur / Richard
Tillinghast.
        p.   cm.—(Poets on poetry)
    ISBN 0-472-09570-6 (hardcover : alk. paper). — ISBN 0-472-06570-X
(pbk. : alk. paper)
    1. Lowell, Robert, 1917–1977. 2. Poets, American—20th century—
Biography. I. Title. II. Series.
PS3523.O89Z885   1995
811'.52—dc20
[B]   95-13706
                                                                    CIP

*Grateful acknowledgment is made to the following journals for permission
to reprint previously published materials.*

Gettysburg Review for "The Vagaries of a Literary Reputation," *Gettysburg Review* 6, no. 3 (Summer 1993), 441–52.

New England Review for "The Wristwatch Is Taken from the Wrist," *New England Review* 16, no. 3 (Summer 1994), 54–63.

Sewanee Review for "Damaged Grandeur: The Life of Robert Lowell," *Sewanee Review* 102, no. 1 (Winter 1994), 121–31.

Virginia Quarterly Review for "Robert Lowell at Harvard," *Virginia Quarterly Review* 71, no. 1 (Winter 1995), 86–100.

Every effort has been made to trace the ownership of all copyrighted materials in this book and to obtain permission for their use.

for
William Alfred

voi, quando nel mondo ad ora ad ora
m'insegnavate come l'uom s'eterna

Contents

Introduction

One wishes heaven had less solemnity:
a sensual table
with five half-filled bottles of red wine
set round the hectic carved roast—
Bohemia for ourselves
and the familiars of a lifetime
charmed to communion by resurrection—

"The Withdrawal"

One of my reasons for writing a book about Robert Lowell at this time is the hope of introducing into the discussion of poetry in the United States an idea or two that seem to have dropped out of sight. In this book I quote from Helen Vendler's memoir, "Lowell in the Classroom," in which she talks about his strikingly personal approach to the poets he read and taught.* "[His] remarks," Vendler comments, "were indistinguishable from those Lowell might have made about a friend or an acquaintance; the poets *were* friends or acquaintances; he knew them from their writing better than most of us knew others from life. This, in the end, seems to me the best thing Lowell did for his students."

In France since the 1950s—following the lead of Roland Barthes, and later, of Michel Foucault—and in the United States since the 1970s, literary criticism has set itself the aim of erasing the author as an entity and treating the "text" as a

---

*Most of the reminiscences I quote in these essays come from *Robert Lowell: Interviews and Memoirs,* ed. Jeffrey Meyers (Ann Arbor: University of Michigan Press, 1988).

bloodless, authorless orphan. The work of art is then approached with what Frederick Crews, in *The Critics Bear It Away*, has called a spirit of "aggressive demystification." In these pages I speak not to literary theorists—who, if they notice this book at all, will regard it as "belletristic" and retro—but to the community of poets and readers of poetry, in hopes of encouraging this community to take back into their own hands the criticism and evaluation of the art. Among poetry's familiars there is room at the table, around the half-finished bottles of wine and the rare, hacked-at roast, for gossip, dispute, causerie, and might-have-beens. In a critical milieu where positive dislike of literature is considered a virtue, those who value poetry need to assert themselves. The theorists have their own agenda, one that offers poetry little nurture. Good luck to them! They leave our story now.

"My thinking is talking to you," Lowell wrote in a late poem to his friend Peter Taylor, emphasizing the personal quality of his poetic discourse. This emphasis contradicts a tendency, dating from the early days of Modernism, and particularly popular with the New Critics, to evoke "the speaker" of a poem, to avoid at all costs the idea that the speaker may be the same person as the author. Student poets in MFA workshops are offended by the very presumption that the speaking voice in their poems may represent some version of their own voices. They react in a spirit of almost doctrinaire fervor against a sense of personal identification with their own poems.

The habit of automatically distinguishing "the speaker" of a poem from its author—the poetic equivalent of what in the study of grammar is called hypercorrection—inevitably introduces an element of distancing and alienation into the writing process. Few—Lowell least of all—would wish to deny that the self is an indeterminate, shifting entity. And it is good for beginning students of poetry to be reminded that authors often speak through a persona or mask. But are those who automatically evoke "the speaker" perhaps evading responsibility for their own poems, thus lowering the stakes and the tension that charge a poem with the risk and excitement of personal commitment?

Except for a few clearly indicated dramatic monologues,

Lowell's poems are personal expressions with a distinct voice. The personal voice also predominates in the work of another poet who will often be mentioned in this book, Elizabeth Bishop. These two poets' willingness to take center stage is part of what gives their work its power. Read Bishop's "One Art" and see whether you feel moved to evoke "the speaker" when she says

> I lost my mother's watch. And look! my last, or
> next-to-last, of three loved houses went.
> The art of losing isn't hard to master.

Thoreau speaks of something slightly different, but to the point, when he says on the first page of *Walden:* "In most books, the *I*, or first person, is omitted; in this it will be retained; that, in respect to egotism, is the main difference. We commonly do not remember that it is, after all, always the first person that is speaking." In these pages I shall often speak in the first person. I have tried to write the kind of book I most enjoy reading: personal, full of anecdote, trying to go to the heart of the matter, making judgments freely, while avoiding literary jargon like bad meat.

This book, a series of reflections on the life and work of Robert Lowell, does not attempt a narrative account of the life. For that the reader will have to turn to Ian Hamilton's *Robert Lowell: A Biography*—flawed and unsatisfactory, but the first full-scale story of the poet's life. Paul Mariani's new biography is a more sympathetic portrait. If I quote freely from Lowell's poems, it is because I want them to stand before the reader's eye when she or he considers my interpretations. But this book does not pretend to be a comprehensive study of the poetry. I have allowed myself the liberty of omitting discussions of large parts of Lowell's *oeuvre*—another day I hope to try to do justice to *Lord Weary's Castle*—and of freely skipping around from one poem to another.

I have assembled here, interwoven with my own observations, an *omnium gatherum* of brief quotations from those who knew Lowell, to give a fully rounded sense of what he was like as a person. I especially hope this book will reach younger readers of poetry for whom Lowell is a "name" they have heard about but have not read thoroughly. May he live in these pages!

Damaged Grandeur, with its eight essays, has a simple plan, but a plan nevertheless. Here is a brief preview of each essay:

The first essay, "Lowell at Harvard," is a personal memoir of the man I knew as a teacher and friend. Illuminating parallels may be drawn between Lowell's personal style and his literary style. His ambivalent rebellion against family tradition and "good" taste informs my discussion of the *Life Studies* poem "Sailing Home from Rapallo." The apprenticeship he served with the Southern poets John Crowe Ransom and Allen Tate might, in a young poet from the South, be seen as submission to tradition. But in a young poet from New England, this choice of masters was further evidence of his determination to rebel. Examining Lowell's handling of family heirlooms in *Life Studies* and earlier, in *Lord Weary's Castle,* this essay explores the headstrong young Bostonian's complex struggle with New England tradition. As a son, as a lover, as a poet, Lowell took to competition the way a Labrador takes to retrieval. I describe a memorable lunch he and I had with James Dickey, whom many considered to be his chief rival. The essay proceeds to a discussion of Lowell's divided political self.

Next, "The Vagaries of a Literary Reputation" traces the history of Lowell's reputation from its high-water mark in the mid-sixties to its current doldrums. To speak of Lowell's poetry at all is to speak of the grip that politics held on his imagination. The gift he brought to the Left as spokesman and critic was the gift of historical perspective: the ability to see the Kennedys as Plutarch might have, or Martin Luther King's assassination as Freud might have in *Civilization and Its Discontents.* My treatment of "Memories of West Street and Lepke" focuses on Lowell's attunement with the *Zeitgeist,* his gift for memorable phrase-making, and his identification with men of power. Lowell's engagement with the world we call "real" has made him, as I shall argue throughout this book, unmalleable stuff for deconstructionists and postmodernists.

But his engagement with the world allies him with William Carlos Williams, Robert Frost, and Seamus Heaney rather than with Wallace Stevens and John Ashbery as a poet of reality rather than philosophy.

"Damaged Grandeur" is biographical; it addresses the sense of largeness or greatness that was the most remarkable thing about Lowell, both as poet and person—this is the "grandeur" of the book's title. Lowell's presumption of greatness carried with it an ability to communicate his enthusiasms to his readers, so that they came to share his preoccupations. From adolescence on, Lowell could bend other people to his way of thinking. Here, because Ian Hamilton's biography has become the context in which most people who did not know Lowell in the flesh have come to know him in print, I evaluate his version of Lowell in some detail. Hamilton presents a case history, not a life. What was remarkable about Lowell's manic-depressive condition was not the fact of the illness, but his resilience and determination in fighting his way clear of it. The question of luck arises: I have often marveled that one person's life could have so much good luck and bad luck inextricably intertwined. This essay also explores Lowell's fascination with power, in both the political and the personal realm. His own manic identification with tyrants, which gave him insight into power politics, became a limitation because he tended to see the *res publica* as an extension of his own personality.

"Robert Lowell Midstream: 'What Next, What Next,'" gives readings of several poems from *For the Union Dead*, the best book Lowell wrote after *Life Studies*, which was where the steel of his genius struck the flint of his times. My method here is explication: I look in detail at six poems, "The Old Flame," "The Lesson," "Those Before Us," "The Drinker," "For the Union Dead," and "The Flaw," frequently comparing them to poems from the book that immediately preceded it, and even glancing as far back as *Lord Weary's Castle*.

That *Life Studies* is the high-water mark of Lowell's writing life is the assumption running through my discussion of his poems. I refer to the poems in this collection more often than to any other part of Lowell's life work. The book has been written about so often and so well, however, that I feel no need to cover old ground or to give a comprehensive reading—which would in any case be impossible in a book of this length. The section of M. L. Rosenthal's book, *The New Poets*, entitled "Robert Lowell and 'Confessional' Poetry," stands up remarkably well after twenty-five years, and I recommend it to any student of Lowell's poems. Rosenthal's remarks, which I did not recall from my earlier reading of his essay on *Life Studies*, about the "forays" of Commander Billy Harkness, spouting doggerel and lampooning Lowell's poet-cousin Amy Lowell, are particularly illuminating: "They add up to the drowning of Lowell senior's deeper but unrealized sensitivity as a man by the extrovert virility of his successful friend who, incidentally and innocently, is at the same time deriding the life of sensibility and its poetic manifestation in particular."

I summarize my overall sense of *Life Studies* before going on to the book that follows it. While *For the Union Dead* lacks the vibrancy, accessibility, and brilliant overall conception of *Life Studies*, it is not the falling-off that most critics have considered it. It is a subtler, more mature book than its predecessor, well worth the effort involved in puzzling out some of its riddle-like knots of meaning.

If my essay on *Life Studies* applies the microscope, the next essay backs off and looks at Lowell through a wide-angle lens. "Mad Ireland hurt you into poetry," W. H. Auden wrote in his elegy "In Memory of W. B. Yeats," and the idea is much bandied about that the hostility contemporary America shows to poetry is responsible for mortally wounding this generation of poets. Lowell calls them "my unhealthy generation" and remarks mordantly, "their lives never stopped stopping." One of the puzzles of our time, often discussed by those who discuss such things, is what caused the madness, suffering, and suicides of Lowell's "Tragic Generation," many of them his close friends, some of them his students.

To the sad and familiar list—Berryman, Jarrell, Schwartz, Roethke, Sexton, Plath—we must now, having read Brett C. Millier's biography, *Elizabeth Bishop: Life and the Memory of It*, add this most exquisite poet who, differing from the others mostly in her old-fashioned and admirable sense of privacy, managed, during her lifetime and with a fair degree of success, to keep her drinking, her sexual preferences, and her unhappiness to herself. At least she didn't snivel as John Berryman did, becoming the lugubrious official mourner, striking poses like "This world is gradually becoming a place / where I do not care to be any more. Can Delmore die?" There is sharpness as well as humor in Lowell's remark in his poem "For John Berryman" from *Day by Day:* "I used to want to live / to avoid your elegy."

Lowell was perhaps the most psychically wounded of them all, and suicide was a constant temptation. Obviously his manic-depressive illness was tremendously painful to him, physically as well as emotionally, as one can feel in these words from "Skunk Hour": "I hear / my ill-spirit sob in each blood cell." There is considerable heroism in the way he resisted the temptation to end it all. In his Foreword to Sylvia Plath's *Ariel* he writes: "In her lines, I often hear the serpent whisper, 'Come, if only you had the courage, you too could have my rightness, audacity and ease of inspiration.' But most of us will turn back. These poems are playing Russian roulette with six cartridges in the cylinder, a game of 'chicken,' the wheels of both cars locked and unable to swerve." It was a terrible conflict for him, and his life was an intermittent struggle, with little respite, to conquer his illness. He must have often asked himself, as he does in *Day by Day:* "Is getting well ever an art, / or art a way to get well?"

I proceed to a discussion of Lowell's late work, specifically his last three books, *For Lizzie and Harriet, The Dolphin,* and *Day by Day,* bypassing in the process important works such as *Near the Ocean* and *Imitations.* In retrospect it is clear—to me at least—that Lowell had "peaked" well before he published the unrhymed fourteen-line poems that make up *History, The Dolphin,* and *For Lizzie and Harriet.* Few readers, in fact, list these poems among their favorites, and I suspect they are seldom read, which is too bad, because there is much to be gained from reading them, even when one doesn't like them much. Leaving *History* for another day, or to other commentators, I have devoted the sixth essay to *For Lizzie and Harriet* and the seventh to *The Dolphin.*

The publishing history of these two books is of more than passing interest, because they began as one—in *Notebook 1967–68*. Lowell later decided to organize the contents of this one volume, along with additional poems, into the three mentioned above. This represented an effort not only to segregate his musings on the *res publica* from the story of his private life, but even to separate his life with Elizabeth Hardwick and his daughter Harriet from his new life with his third wife, Caroline Blackwood, her children, and their son Sheridan. The fourteen-line, unrhymed "sonnets" in which the sequences are written posed formal problems that turned out to be as much a hindrance as a help. Lowell became entangled in the minutiae of revision. In the private poems he never mastered the problems of propriety and even of morality inherent in the material.

Lowell explores his powerful attraction to a woman, and to women, in both volumes, but especially in *The Dolphin*. In "Going to and fro" from *For the Union Dead,* he wrote, pairing himself with Satan:

> Ah Lucifer!
> how often you wanted your fling
> with those French girls, Mediterranean
> luminaries, Mary, Myrtho, Isis—
> as far out as the sphynx!
> The love that moves the stars
>
> moved you!

These lines succinctly illustrate how close the erotic and the mythic were for this poet who, as Diane Middlebrook puts it in her biography of Anne Sexton, always "had to be 'in love.'" *The Dolphin,* whatever its shortcomings—and in this chapter I try to articulate my serious reservations about the book—bravely dissects Lowell's conflicted feelings about women, particularly the two women characters in this book.

To me, the biggest question to be asked about Robert Lowell is how he managed to bring such an air of authority to his poems, how it was that at his peak, everything he wrote seemed crucial, "relevant," a must-read. In a letter she wrote Lowell in 1957 after she had read his *Life Studies* in manuscript, Elizabeth Bishop addresses this question:

> And here I must confess (and I imagine most of our contemporaries would confess the same thing) that I am green with envy of your kind of assurance. I feel that I could write in as much detail about my Uncle Artie, say—but what would be the significance? Nothing at all. He became a drunkard, fought with his wife, and spent most of his time fishing . . . and was ignorant as sin. It is sad; slightly more interesting than having an uncle practising law in Schenectady maybe, but that's all. Whereas all you have to do is put down the names! And [the] fact that it seems significant, illustrative, American, etc., gives you, I think, the confidence you display about tackling any idea or theme, *seriously,* in both writing and conversation. In some ways you are the luckiest poet I know!—in some ways not so lucky, either, of course.

Millier, Bishop's biographer, sees fit to scold her for not having the requisite level of political correctness: "It seems not to have occurred to her that Lowell's 'assurance' might have had as much to do with the privileges of gender as of family background."

That person whom Virginia Woolf called "the common reader" always seems destined to be confronted by critics who want to resolve these mysteries by one or another reductive explanatory system. Miller's reductionism is based on gender. Earlier readers, myself included, have used Freud as a key. Lowell was alternately exasperated and amused by the psychoanalytical readings I brought to his poetry in my 1970 Harvard dissertation. He felt some of the same reservations about the Freudian emphasis of Alan Williamson's brilliant 1974 book, *Pity the Monsters: The Political Vision of Robert Lowell.*

In his later years Lowell did not experience a change in gender, nor did he become any less upper class. Why, then, did his poetry lose its air of authority? Why did his autobiographical writing become less compelling? I have no easy answers to these questions, except to say what is obvious, that it has everything to do with those elusive qualities called voice and authenticity. I try to consider these matters in detail in the sixth and seventh essays.

The mutual influence, the give-and-take between two writers as miraculously gifted as Lowell and Bishop, continued throughout their lifetimes. The late David Kalstone's account of this poetic friendship, along with Bishop's daughterlike apprenticeship to and friendship with Marianne Moore, is the subject of his indispensable posthumous book, *Becoming a Poet*. Despite the characteristic self-deprecation of her comments about her Uncle Artie, Bishop was emboldened by the prose of "91 Revere Street" to write the life of her Uncle Artie in "Memories of Uncle Neddy," which is a priceless character study—and more. In addition to the preternatural ability to bring a character and a milieu to life in print, Bishop shared Lowell's knack of using a deftly sketched character to refract light onto her own personality.

The last essay addresses itself to *Day by Day*, Lowell's last book. He had clearly emerged from the tone of self-induced hypnotism that characterizes the "sonnets" at their worst. The book has flashes of clarity, and its valedictory air and retrospective look at earlier writings and old friends moves one to tears. In addition, the visual element was, throughout this poet's work, prominent, and nowhere more vivid than in *Day by Day*, which explores a visually centered aesthetic, calling for "description without significance," amounting to an attempt to write poetry that would ultimately defy interpretation. Throughout his career Lowell opened himself fully to the reader, and his self-doubts in this volume are agonizing. One feels that in his strong awareness of death, he anticipated that this book would be his last. I wish I could claim that it is better than it is. That Lowell's death in 1977 deprived him of the chance to continue in the direction he had begun in *Day by Day* must be a great sorrow to any reader of poetry.

Robert Lowell at Harvard

Antiques and quarrels from "91 Revere Street" mix in memory with Kentucky bluegrass and whitewashed fences seen from the back seat of my father's white Buick. My parents were driving me from Memphis to Cambridge in 1962 to begin graduate school. I was reading *Life Studies* for the first time. The angst, the vulnerability, the exposed nerves of the author of that often harrowing book led me to expect someone other than the man I was about to meet.

Physically, Robert Lowell gave an impression of force, with strong shoulders and an unusually large head—not a head that revealed the skull and hinted at the brain, as with his mentor Allen Tate, but one, rather, that gave a powerful but awkward, elemental impression, making one think simultaneously of a bull and a creature of the sea. Though he had been a footballer at both St. Mark's and Kenyon, where he played varsity tackle, fishing was later in life the one sport he found meaningful. He was born under the constellation Pisces.

Water was his element. I can think of no other poet who evoked the sea so often and so tellingly. Fish, gulls, whales, turtles, seals appear again and again in his work. The dolphin of his later work was both muse and self:

> Any clear thing that blinds us with surprise,
> your wandering silences and bright trouvailles,
> dolphin let loose to catch the flashing fish. . . .

These lines—whose unlikely rhyme, *surprise / trouvailles,* itself surprises—speak to the restlessness, the search for novelty, the need to reinvent himself periodically that characterize

Lowell's entire career. It was this impulse which led him to invent the personal style of *Life Studies*—"the biggest change *in myself* [my italics] perhaps I ever made or will." The sea for Lowell was an eternal present, an emblem of the life force as he saw it, brutal and destructive: "The ocean, grinding stones," he wrote in "Near the Ocean," "can only speak the present tense; / nothing will age, nothing will last." The sea was the expressive agent for his Jeremiah-like and frightening zeal as early as his first major work, "The Quaker Graveyard at Nantucket," with its heavily cadenced patterns of sound:

> Sea-gulls blink their heavy lids
> Seaward. The winds' wings beat upon the stones,
> Cousin, and scream for you and the claws rush
> At the sea's throat and wring it in the slush
> Of this old Quaker graveyard where the bones
> Cry out in the long night for the hurt beast
> Bobbing by Ahab's whaleboats in the East.

The surface he presented to the world when I met him seventeen years after the publication of this poem was more composed. I picture him during the years I knew him at Harvard: in the penthouse seminar room at the top of Jose Luis Sert's Holyoke Center, where he taught a class. Some Rothkos, with their mauve and rotting-earth colors, brooded on the walls there. Or in his rooms at Quincy House, or in the basement seminar room there, where he held his "office hours," a free-ranging seminar on poems brought in by the diverse group of writers who came on Wednesday mornings—Jean Valentine, Frank Bidart, Helen Chasin, Heather McHugh, Alan Williamson, Roger Rosenblatt, Sidney Goldfarb, Robert Grenier, Lloyd Schwartz, and others. The office hours consisted of two or three hours of practical criticism interlaced with free-ranging conversation about poetry. After "office hours" one or two of us would accompany him to his favorite restaurant, the Iruña, for vodka martinis and Spanish food.

To speak, in today's critical parlance, of the "death of the author," would have made no more sense to Lowell than to say the person you were playing tennis with was dead. He openly admired and was on intimate terms with his favorite poets from the past. "Tennyson is an intense, moody, clumsy young man with enormous metrical skill," Judith Baumel reports him remarking. "Pound, who loathed him, has a Tennysonian splendor." It was in Lowell's company that I first understood what Shakespeare was getting at in his sonnets when he wrote that poetry could immortalize—or what Dante meant when he paid tribute in Hell to his master Brunetto Latini (in Lowell's own translation), "when in the world, from hour to hour you taught / me how a man becomes eternal."

Helen Vendler's reminiscence, "Lowell in the Classroom," which I invoked in the Introduction, is worth quoting at some length, because she kept notes on his comments on nineteenth-century poetry:

> Lowell began his classes on each successive poet with an apparently indolent, speculative, and altogether selective set of remarks on the poet's life and writing; the poet appeared as a man with a temperament, a set of difficulties, a way of responding, a vocation, prejudices . . .|. he gave [his students] the sense . . . of a life, a spirit, a mind, and a set of occasions from which writing issues—a real life, a real mind, fixed in historical circumstance and quotidian abrasions. . . . What his privileged students heard was original discourse; what they experienced was the amplitude of response stirred by past poetry—which, in Lowell's hands, always seemed poetry of the present—by a poet who had earned his place "on the slopes of Parnassus." It was a response in which familiarity and reverence went hand in hand, in which technique and vision were indissoluble; it made the appearance of poetry in life seem as natural as any other action.

He slouches in a leather chair, a penny loafer dangling from one foot, shoulders scrunched up toward his massive head— his hands framing a point in the air, held up before his face as though to protect it from attack, now and then righting the black-rimmed glasses that kept sliding down the bridge of his thick nose, one of many True cigarettes between his fingers, worrying away a digressive train of thought. With his broad face and "oval Lowell smile," he bore an uncanny resemblance to the pictures of both Amy Lowell and James Russell Lowell in the *American Heritage Dictionary*. The jaunty, pastel shirt-and-tie combinations—the opposite of traditional—that he would sometimes wear made one cringe, yet they were typical of one who loathed conventional "good taste" and delighted in things that were jarring and vivid. When Lowell writes of Randall Jarrell, "You felt that even your choice in neckties wounded him," it's easy to see that Jarrell must have been wounded often in Lowell's company.

His rebelliousness against family tradition and the sedate "good" taste that felt like a stranglehold surfaces disturbingly in this account of his departure from Italy, bringing his mother's body home, in the *Life Studies* poem called "Sailing Home from Rapallo":

> When I embarked from Italy with my Mother's body,
> the whole shoreline of the *Golfo di Genova*
> was breaking into fiery flower.
> The crazy yellow and azure sea-sleds
> blasting like jack-hammers across
> the *spumante*-bubbling wake of our liner,
> recalled the clashing colors of my Ford.
> Mother travelled first-class in the hold;
> her *Risorgimento* black and gold casket
> was like Napoleon's at the *Invalides*.

What shocks one here is that the exuberance of the flowers on shore and the scene in the harbor mirror the bereaved son's inner celebration of his mother's death. The "*spumante*-bubbling wake" of the ship suggests a glass raised in celebration. "The clashing colors of my Ford" evoke adolescent independence and self-assertion, while at the same time reminding us of the car's role in the mad poet's pursuit of his dark obsessions in "Skunk Hour," where

> One dark night,
> my Tudor Ford climbed the hill's skull;
> I watched for love-cars. Lights turned down,
> they lay together, hull to hull,
> where the graveyard shelves on the town. . . .
> My mind's not right.

The imperial casket had of course been Lowell's own choice: "I went to Genoa and bought Mother a black-and-gold baroque casket that would have been suitable for burying her hero Napoleon at Les Invalides," he writes in the prose reminiscence "Near the Unbalanced Aquarium." The casket was a way of honoring what he perceived as his mother's own heroic fantasy of herself—a fantasy that in his manic phases had become his own. The preparations he made, the way he responded to her death, show that he was being propelled into another bout of insanity: "When Mother died, I began to feel tireless, madly sanguine, menaced, and menacing. I entered the Payne-Whitney Clinic for 'all those afflicted in mind.' "

The lines that follow deliver a sobering corrective to the gaudy colors and unnaturally high spirits of the verse paragraph from "Sailing Home from Rapallo" I quoted above:

> While the passengers were tanning
> on the Mediterranean in deck-chairs,
> our family cemetery in Dunbarton
> lay under the White Mountains
> in the sub-zero weather.
> The graveyard's soil was changing to stone—
> so many of its deaths had been midwinter.
> Dour and dark against the blinding snowdrifts,
> its black brook and fir trunks were as smooth as masts.
> A fence of iron spear-hafts
> black-bordered its mostly Colonial grave-slates.

To say that these lines reveal the depressive side of Lowell's mania demonstrates the inadequacy of psychological terminology in painting the rich complexity of psychological and emotional states. But clearly something like what is crudely defined by those terms is at work here. The preferred contemporary usage, "bipolar disorder," hits somewhat closer to the mark.

The two passages are a wonderful study in contrast: spring and winter, "crazy yellow and azure" as opposed to black and white—heat and cold, flowers and snow, water and stone, frantic liveliness and the stasis of death. The motor-powered sea-sleds likened to jack-hammers recall Lowell's use of the same figure in "Colloquy in Black Rock" from *Lord Weary's Castle:* "Here the jack-hammer jabs into the ocean; / My heart, you race and stagger and demand / More blood-gangs for your nigger-brass percussions." This physically jarring and debilitating rush must have been what Lowell's manic states felt like.

An image like "nigger-brass," appropriating a racial slur and internalizing it, points forward to the self-denigrating images in another poem based on one of his manic attacks, "A Mad Negro Soldier Confined at Munich." The sentence "Each subnormal boot- / black heart is pulsing to its ant-egg dole" gives guilt and self-loathing a social framework.

The cemetery, by contrast, has tremendous dignity. Transience turns to permanence there, where "The graveyard's soil was changing to stone." The last four lines return to the Miltonic cadences and elevated style of "The Quaker Graveyard at Nantucket," with the monosyllabic Anglo-Saxon alliteration of "dour and dark" and "black brook," which echo the impressive spondees of the early style.

That Lowell's speech bore subtle but clearly recognizable traces of a Southern accent—much remarked-upon by those who met him—was only one of many paradoxes, but it said something about this complex and often contradictory person. Perhaps the accent had rubbed off in the course of many years of marriage to Elizabeth Hardwick, who was born in Kentucky. I fancy, though, he picked it up from the crowd of Tennesseans and Kentuckians, teachers and friends, whom he had met in his early twenties when he left Harvard after his sophomore year to study at Kenyon and LSU: Allen Tate, John Ransom, Randall Jarrell, Peter Taylor, "Red" Warren. Lowell saw a certain symmetry in the circumstances that had brought me—a Tennessean who as a student of Andrew Lytle's and a friend of Peter and Eleanor Taylor's had been imbued in the Agrarian tradition at Sewanee—to New England and Harvard to study with him. In the brief prose piece, "Visiting the Tates," which Lowell wrote for an issue of the *Sewanee Review* honoring Allen Tate, he has this to say about his first exposure to the South's sense of American history *chez* the poet who had been one of his substitute fathers:

> I began to discover what I had never known. I, too, was part of a legend. I was Northern, disembodied, a Platonist, a puritan, an abolitionist. Tate handed me a hand-painted, defiantly gingersnap-thin edition of his *The Mediterranean and Other Poems*. He quoted a stanza from Holmes's "Chambered Nautilus"—"rather beyond the flight of your renowned Uncle." I realized that the old deadweight of poor J. R. Lowell was now an asset. Here, like the battered Confederacy, he still lived and was history.

Perhaps, in turn, it was Lowell's tutelage that brought it to my attention in Cambridge that I was Southern. To me the softness of his Tennessee *l*'s was reassuringly familiar at Harvard in the sixties, where I found that my own Southern accent was usually greeted with hostility. Probably Lowell's accent was a sign of rebellion against a New England heritage he both rejected and thoroughly embodied—a heritage that for him carried a load of guilt and was inextricable from his feelings toward his family. The connection between his conflicts with his father and the exceptions he took to upper-class New England culture surfaces most baldly in "Rebellion" for *Lord Weary's Castle*. "There was rebellion, father," the poem begins, "when the mock / French windows slammed and you hove backward, rammed / Into your heirlooms."

The poem fails, according to Steven Gould Axelrod, in his book *Robert Lowell: Life and Art*, because it "seeks to masquerade personal confession as historical and mythic statement, a disguise that serves only to confuse the poem. Lowell's adolescent assault on his father is inflated into an obscure parable of patricide and damnation, heavy with overtones from *Job* . . . and American history." Perhaps taken out of the context of Lowell's complete *oeuvre*, the poem might be considered a failure. Reading it with the later work in mind, however, it fascinatingly foreshadows the *Life Studies* material. The heirlooms of this poem are the same houseful of furniture that symbolize the heavy weight of the past in the prose piece "91

Revere Street"—presided over by a portrait of Lowell's remote ancestor, Major Mordecai Myers:

> Great-great-Grandfather Myers had never frowned down in judgment on a Salem witch. There was no allegory in his eyes, no *Mayflower*. Instead he looked peacefully at his sideboard, his cut-glass decanters, his cellaret—the worldly bosom of the Mason-Myers mermaid engraved on a silver-plated urn. If he could have spoken, Mordecai would have said, "My children, my blood, accept graciously the loot of your inheritance. We are all dealers in used furniture."

The incident itself, when he knocked his father down, furious over his father's interference in his engagement at the age of nineteen to a girl his parents considered unsuitable, haunted Lowell for the rest of his life, and he wrote about it more than once; but this was his first attempt at it. An account of the aftermath, given by his close friend Frank Parker to Lowell's biographer Ian Hamilton, suggests what an impossible person Charlotte Lowell must have been:

> If you had a German shepherd, taking care of it and getting the best food and care and so on, and then it bit you, wouldn't you shoot it? Or wouldn't you have it shut out—that's what she said to me. Anger, fear, you know. Mr. Lowell was nowhere to be seen. He was nursing his jaw.

Obscure and confused the ending of the poem may very well be. But there is no "disguise," no "masquerade" here. Myth and history were not, for Lowell, obfuscations. They were deeply felt realities.

Lowell's biographer Ian Hamilton records Jackie Kennedy's lending Bobby Kennedy the marked copy of Plutarch's *Lives* Lowell had given her. According to Grey Gowrie, "Bobby was rather funny about Cal [Lowell's nickname from boarding school]. He sort of admired him but at the same time he thought his politics were absolutely bananas." Looking back, there is something amusing as well as poignant about the exchange Hamilton describes between Lowell and Robert Kennedy, who was ten years Lowell's junior. They were discussing

The Education of Henry Adams. "Bobby suddenly got up and excused himself. Lowell followed him right to the door of the bathroom, still reading. Bobby shut the door and said 'If you don't mind.' Lowell said: 'If you were Louis XIV you wouldn't mind.' "

Plutarch comes up in Lowell's elegy for Robert Kennedy, as do the clean white shirts Kennedy changed into several times a day on the campaign trail. The poem places the assassinated younger brother in the archaic context established by the reference to Louis XIV I have just quoted:

> Doom was woven in your nerves, your shirt,
> woven in the great clan; they too were loyal,
> and you too more than loyal to them, to death.
> For them like a prince, you daily left your tower
> to walk through dirt in your best cloth. Untouched,
> alone in my Plutarchan bubble, I miss
> you, you out of Plutarch, made by hand—
> forever approaching our maturity.

Nothing is more essential to an appreciation of Lowell's sensibility than to understand that when he compared Robert Kennedy with Louis XIV, it was because Louis XIV was more real to him than anyone in the world of contemporary politics, Plutarch's *Lives* more immediate than the front page of the *New York Times.* Patricide lies just beneath the surface of the poem's action. When, in the poem, Lowell "broke the chimney flintlock on [his father's] skull," that flintlock bears all the burden of the Puritan Indian-killers and the rapacious Yankee merchants of his view of New England history:

> Behemoth and Leviathan
> Devoured our mighty merchants. None could arm
> Or put to sea. O father, on my farm
> I added field to field
> And I have sealed
> An everlasting pact
> With Dives to contract
> The world that spreads in pain;
> But the world spread
> When the clubbed flintlock broke my father's brain.

One gets a better sense of what all of this meant to Lowell from Randall Jarrell's essay, "From the Kingdom of Necessity" printed in *Poetry and the Age:*

> The poems understand the world as a sort of conflict of opposites. In this struggle one opposite is that cake of custom, in which all of us lie embedded like lungfish—the stasis or inertia of the stubborn self, the obstinate persistence in evil that is damnation. Into this realm of necessity the poems push everything that is closed, turned inward, incestuous, that blinds or binds: the Old Law, imperialism, militarism, capitalism, Calvinism, Authority, the Father, the "proper Bostonians," the rich. . . . But struggling within this like leaven, falling to it like light, is everything that is free or open, that grows or is willing to change.

The son who connives with the world of materialism, who has "added field to field," has for a time thrown in his lot with what Jarrell calls "the Kingdom of Necessity." This accommodation was one of many similar ones Lowell would make throughout his life—an instance of which was his purchase of 239 Marlborough Street in 1955 as part of a desire to set himself up as Boston Brahmin, be accepted back into the Episcopal Church, and live the upper-middle-class life his ancestors had enjoyed. "We're having a good fall," he jokingly wrote Peter Taylor, "and feel very lordly and pretentious in our new Boston house. . . . It's not really little and not at all unpretentious, and we despise everyone whose nerve for cities has failed, all country people, all suburbanites, and all people who live in apartments." His uneasiness with this stance comes out in a letter to William Carlos Williams: "We might even become Boston worthies, if it weren't for the worm of life in us."

Rebellion, "the worm of life," the need for change without which life was not worth living. It is instructive and even frightening to realize that to accomplish these things, an assault on his father, a symbolic murder, was called for. This is how Jarrell puts it:

> In "Rebellion" the son seals "an everlasting pact / With Dives to *contract* / The world that *spreads* in pain"; but at last he rebels

against his father and his father's New England commercial theocracy, and "the world *spread* / When the clubbed flintlock broke my father's brain." The italicized words ought to demonstrate how explicitly, at times, these poems formulate the world in the terms that I have used.

A poem like "Rebellion" shows how dangerously "serious" Lowell could be. For those who knew him in the 1940s, the surface impression was simply that he was a remarkably humorless young man. Clearly the madness that would later manifest itself in cycles of manic attacks followed by depressive entrenchments was already gestating. The torture and enervation (a word that recurs in his poetry) of recurrent mental breakdowns, and perhaps worse, the treatment for them, had not left him, in the early sixties, with a sanguine attitude toward life: in *For the Union Dead* he writes of enervation: "the downward glide / and bias of existing wrings us dry." Yet in his late forties and early fifties, one could see him unbend and mellow as he came to a slow acceptance of the world and himself. In *Day by Day* he wrote (of his mother):

> Your exaggerating humor,
> the opposite of deadpan,
> the opposite of funny to a son,
> is mine now—

A gifted alien, a stranger to the ordinary, sometimes hardly human at all, he relished broad humor, the ridiculous, the common. In his healthy periods, I think he was often overcome with joy at the feeling of being "normal," and thus delighted in the obvious. The exaggerating element in his humor, which could be charming or tiresome, was the counterpart of his extravagant poetic style.

Once during the term at Harvard, perhaps during 1967, I got Lowell and James Dickey, who was giving poetry readings at Harvard, Boston College, and elsewhere, together for lunch. Circumstances, and the two men's temperaments, had cast them as rivals. Peter Davison, in a widely noted article in the *Atlantic Monthly*, had just coupled them as the nation's two leading poets. While differing greatly in background and style, they had more in common than was immediately obvious. Their genius, the scope of their ambition, their boundless energy, and a radical originality set them apart from most of their contemporaries. Both were hypersensitive to criticism; both had recently been the subjects of full-scale critical broadsides by Robert Bly in his influential magazine, *The Sixties*.

We met at Chez Dreyfus on Church Street in Cambridge. Dickey and I had been drinking beer since breakfast, and had just come from my writing class, where he had put in a splendid guest appearance. Lowell was not supposed to be drinking, as alcohol was incompatible with the lithium pills he took for his illness. He made an exception (not unusual) for the occasion; food was soon forgotten, vodka flowed. Sparring between the two poets was in evidence, some of it good-natured, some of it not.

Dickey, who at that time hunted with bow and arrow, pulled up his shirt under the disapproving eye of our French waiter and showed us a large bandage on his back. Then he started telling us about a recent trip to the West Virginia wilderness. It was a good story. Having stopped to drink from a mountain stream, he had looked up just in time to see a huge bear reared up on its hind legs, making straight for him. Just as the bear had attacked, raking his back and shoulder with razor-sharp claws, Dickey got off an arrow that killed it. "But the bear wasn't dead, Jim," Lowell interrupted, himself suddenly bearlike, myopically clearing his way with gesturing hands, laughing as he always did at the remark he was about to make: "When you got back to your office, the bear was sitting at your desk. It was Robert Bly."

Lowell was not easily convinced by hasty political solutions to complex problems. One irony of his career was his position in the sixties as a poetic spokesman for the Left (not that he didn't want it and work for it). In this profoundly divided person, radicalism was balanced by a rock-ribbed, atavistic sense of tradition. It is well known that Lowell was a Conscientious Objector in World War II, protesting the Allied bombing of civilians at Dresden and elsewhere, and that he went to jail for it. Yet earlier he had tried to enlist in the Navy but had been rejected because of poor eyesight. In all events, the divisions in his own personality afforded him an unusually good opportunity to understand both sides of most political issues.

In 1969 Lowell was offered a visiting professorship for the following spring in the English Department of the University of California at Berkeley. I was on the faculty there at the time, having left Harvard the previous year, and I backed up the offer with a glowing description of the political struggle at Berkeley and of the overall atmosphere of the place. Those were heady times; it really did look as though the walls were about to come down. My enthusiasm was genuine, as was my naiveté. Lowell used my letter as the basis of a poem, "The Revolution," in *History*. (Anyone who has had occasion to study Lowell's methods of quotation will know that with him, poetic license was a way of life.) Whatever its relationship to what I wrote in my letter—I can hardly say after twenty-six years—the quoted part of the poem reads:

> "We're in a prerevolutionary situation
> at Berkeley, an incredible, refreshing relief
> from your rather hot-house, good prep-school Harvard riots.
> The main thing is our exposure to politics;
> whether this a priori will determine
> the revolutionary's murder in the streets,
> or the death of the haves by the have-nots, I don't know;
> but anyway you should be in on it—
> only in imagination can we lose the battle."

It's clear that lines five to seven and line nine were Robert Lowell's work. The following excerpt from his reply to my letter gives the flavor of both his warmth and his ironic sense of humor:

> About Berkeley—the big classes, the two public lectures (described to me by Professor Raleigh) are out of my style. Then the being away from home—I don't think I can decide this year about 1971. Still I feel drawn by Berkeley. Maybe less now. Your saying that I "should be in on it" is as tho I were to offer you Castine by saying "we seem likely to have a tidal wave and you should see the morale of a village in danger." I have so

little faith in any of the sides, tho some in some things. Or rather, it's a joy this summer to be back to real life (real rest?) The contentions, the revolution, the counter-revolution, will all come back to me, I cannot doubt it, and perhaps they'll be welcome.

Well, Lizzie and I miss your old visits, and wish you were back.

Affectionately,
Cal

Lowell in Castine, Maine, in his studio, a converted barn by the ocean, painted a hideous aluminum color inside. Him barefoot, wearing a crusty old Harvard blazer, cooking lobsters, and drinking beer like any Bostonian up for the summer. Trying to describe the wind-filled shape of a striped jib while watching a sailboat regatta through binoculars, which he then turns on a rabbit crouched in the dry bracken— fascinated by the blood pulsing through magnified veins in the rabbit's alert pink ears.

Those of us whom good luck led to study writing with Robert Lowell, he taught almost by indirection, yet managed to touch us with a sense of his own struggle for the absolute in poetry. He transmitted a total dedication to the effort of laying words down on the page like a fresh coat of paint. In the tradition of his own youth—of Ford Madox Ford, John Crowe Ransom, and Allen Tate—he showed that a poem "must be tinkered with and recast until one's eyes pop out of one's head." At the same time, he believed that the goal and meaning of writing lay beyond the mere process of writing; he was in his way as much a transcendentalist as Emerson. When the fit took him he was really and truly mad, genuinely menacing—a maniac, if that word describes someone under the spell of mania. I have heard of his unkindnesses, and I don't doubt them, but to me he was always kind and, indeed, helped me through a very low period of my life. To me he was a pure and simple soul trapped by fate in a tragically flawed personality and life.

When I first left Cambridge it was even something of a relief to be away from him. His view of the world was a burden not only to him but to those around him, who learned to see things through his eyes. I went for years without seeing him, except for once, in passing, in London. But when he died—too young, at sixty—I felt that the roof had been ripped off the sky.

The Vagaries of a Literary
Reputation

If any midcentury American poet seemed in the estimation of his contemporaries certain to be read and admired by posterity, surely that poet was Robert Lowell. "Somehow or other, by fair means or foul," Elizabeth Bishop wrote of *Life Studies* (1959), "and in the middle of our worst century so far, we have produced a magnificent poet." Richard Poirier commented around the same time: "Robert Lowell is, by something like a critical consensus, the greatest American poet of the mid-century, probably the greatest poet now writing in English." In the late forties Lowell took American literature by storm, winning the Pulitzer Prize for this first book *Lord Weary's Castle,* and making the established generation of Karl Shapiro, John Frederick Nims, John Ciardi, Howard Moss, and Howard Nemerov look outdated.

Lowell straddled the poetry scene of his day like a colossus—perhaps, in retrospect, to use one of his own favorite adjectives, a "top-heavy" colossus, ripe for a fall. The decline in his reputation since his death from a heart attack in 1977 has been dramatic. Let's go back twenty-five years, however, to the height of his literary eminence. The 2 June 1967 issue of *Time*—featuring on its cover a hideous Sidney Nolan portrait of Lowell, laurels crayoned over his troubled brow—detailed his accumulated achievements. His sixth book of verse, *Near the Ocean,* had recently been published. He was fifty—ten years since "Memories of West Street and Lepke," in which he had made the resounding declaration, "These are the tranquillized, *Fifties,* / and I am forty," providing the decade with an epithet that stuck. Three years before, his dramatic trilogy *The Old Glory*, directed by Jonathan Miller at the American Place Theatre in New York, had won five Obie awards and been adjudged by Robert Brustein "a cultural-poetic masterpiece." His version of Aeschylus' *Prometheus Bound* had just opened at the Yale School of Drama.

Time, reflecting prevailing critical opinion, sounded overwhelmed by Lowell's scope and achievement, as suggested by the subheading, "Man Who Has Everything." "In *Near the Ocean*," *Time* observed in a tone that oscillates between awe and incredulity, "the first few pages bring together Goliath, God, Joan Baez, Cotton Mather, Jesus Christ, Ralph Waldo Emerson, Monteverdi, Trollope, civil rights clergy, Homer, his own New England roots, Calvin, and even the President of the U.S.—seen in the White House swimming pool:

> girdled by his establishment
> this Sunday morning, free to chaff
> his own thoughts with his bear-cuffed staff,
> swimming nude, unbuttoned, sick
> of his ghost-written rhetoric!"
>
> "Waking Early Sunday Morning"

Today no American poet occupies the preeminent position Lowell held in the fifties and sixties. His friend and contemporary Elizabeth Bishop, who died two years after he did, is the admired poet of their generation, while the two most highly thought-of living poets are Seamus Heaney, an Irishman, and Derek Walcott, of Afro-Caribbean extraction. American poetry itself has been gerrymandered into constituencies—reflective of a national trend toward compartmentalization by gender, ethnic group, and life-style.

To name only three contemporary American poets: John Ashbery is admired by readers with a mandarin sensibility who are drawn to his method of elevating indeterminacy of meaning to an aesthetic all its own, which makes him particularly attractive to academic champions of deconstructionism. James Merrill, the most fluent verse-writer of our time, has his own champions, especially among those who enjoy the gossipy dramas of the Ouija-board epic, *The Changing Light at Sandover*. Many feminists revere Adrienne Rich, who strikes other readers as being more arresting as polemicist than as poet. Others might dismiss Rich, Merrill, and Ashbery all three as East Coast elitist. Or as "Eurocentric," in which case one reads Maya Angelou, Ai, Yusef Komunyakaa, Imamu Amiri Baraka, Garrett Hongo, Gary Soto, or Rita Dove. Because no poet today clearly stands out above the crowd, no poet is able to use whatever prestige poetry might have in the service of public issues. Robert Lowell's assurance, the ease with which he assumed a place for poetry in the councils of power, seems unthinkable today.

In his time Lowell was part of the glamorous aura surrounding the Kennedys, appearing on the cover of *Women's Wear Daily* accompanying Jacqueline Kennedy to the first night of William Alfred's acclaimed play *Hogan's Goat*. He thrived on his associations with the world of politics, and not just because of the glamor. The poet had something to contribute to the world of politics, because he brought to contemporary events a historical perspective that politicians often lack. The two public gestures for which he is most remembered are gestures of refusal, both of them handled in a manner consistent with upper-class social protocol. The first proclaimed Lowell a Conscientious Objector during World War I, when he began a letter to Franklin Delano Roosevelt:

> I very much regret that I must refuse the opportunity you offer me in your communication of August 6, 1943, for service in the Armed Forces. . . . You will understand how painful such a decision is for an American whose family traditions, like your own, have always found their fulfillment in maintaining, through responsible participation in both the civil and the military services, our country's freedom and honor.

Lowell's second refusal also took the form of a rejected invitation—though this time the invitation really was to a social event, the White House Festival of the Arts, scheduled for June 1965. Temperamentally ambivalent, Lowell first accepted a telephone invitation to the event. In his letter to Lyndon

Johnson, which the *New York Times* printed on its front page, he wrote:

> After a week's wondering, I have decided that I am conscience-bound to refuse your courteous invitation. . . .We are in danger of imperceptibly becoming an explosive and suddenly chauvinistic nation, and may even be drifting on our way to the last nuclear ruin. . . . I feel I am serving you and our country best by not taking part in the White House Festival of the Arts.

This poet's public gestures were consistent with an attitude he maintained throughout his life, not a stance or a consciously assumed position, but something that was simply part of his character, one that struck those around him as *sui generis*, that drew people to him and made them love him. Criticism—and this applies as much to the out-of-fashion New Criticism of the forties and fifties as it does to today's Post-Structuralism, Deconstruction, etc.—prefers to consider its "texts" authorless. But in reality is it not natural—and desirous—that the artist should influence his contemporaries personally? If the artist happens to be a poet, he will make his public impact through language. In the absence of positive opportunities, Lowell made, through his strategic refusals, a virture of negation. Poetry, to our culture's loss, plays an increasingly smaller role in public life. If one of poetry's traditional functions is, in Mallarmé's phrase, "to purify the language of the tribe," to articulate, in Pope's words, "what oft was thought, but ne'er so well express'd," one may trace the current public deterioration of language partially to the absence of a literary influence in favor of clarity, economy, and grace.

A word used by many who knew the man is "serious." The poet Frank Bidart, a devoted friend who worked closely with Lowell and advised him on revisions during the composition of much of his later work—the poems which would become *History, The Dolphin,* and *For Lizzie and Harriet*—has written: "He once said to me, 'When I'm dead, I don't care what you write about me; all I ask is that it be *serious*.'. . . However courtly or charming, casual or playful he was by turns, in his

art and his personal relationships Lowell was unfashionably—
even, at times, ruthlessly—*serious.*" For a complex set of rea-
sons, Lowell carried with him what Seamus Heaney in a me-
morial address read at St. Luke's Church in London on
5 October 1977, defined as a "nimbus of authority that ringed
his writings and his actions."

It was not simply that he suffered for the words he wrote—
other writers suffer without attaining that hard-won dignity
of the survivor one feels in Lowell. To analyze his aura of
authority would burst the staves of this paragraph, and even
the hoops of this chapter. But everyone who came in contact
with him felt the perhaps indefinable but palpable presence
of authority that Heaney invokes:

> Just as in that older [medieval] dispensation, the order and
> coherence of things was ratified in the person of the prince, so
> in the person of the poetry of Robert Lowell, the whole scope
> and efficacy of the artistic endeavour was exemplified and
> affirmed. And his death shook the frame of poetry. He did not
> pitch his voice at "the public" but he so established the practice
> of art as a moral function within his own life that when he
> turned outward to make gestures against the quality of the life
> of his times, those gestures had been well earned and possessed
> a memorable force.

To say that no poet today writes with comparable moral
force is not to denigrate our contemporaries. For starters, the
changes in our culture may be too complex to allow for the
kinds of generalizations that comparisons between Lowell and
living writers would suggest. Opposition to the Vietnam War
forged a consensus that has since disintegrated. In addition,
the envy engendered among fellow poets by his virtual mo-
nopoly on the limited fame our culture is willing to allocate to
poetry was starting to catch up with Lowell even before the
end of the Vietnam era. More important was that, as early as
Notebook 1967–68, Lowell had already lost the knack of writ-
ing poems like "For the Union Dead," which resonated for a
wide spectrum of readers while remaining true to its author's
own complexity and ambivalence.

Lowell's power as a political poet lay in his knack of becoming one with the *Zeitgeist,* and—despite the many things that made him absolutely unlike anyone else—somehow managing to dramatize himself in his poems as a representative citizen. Lowell was attuned to what Dr. Johnson meant when he said, "Nothing can please many, or please long, but just representations of general nature." The Lowellian version of Keats's Negative Capability is visible throughout his career. Stanley Kunitz has commented in "The Sense of a Life" on his old friend's attunement to the literary climate: "he watched its weather with the diligent attention of a meteorologist, studying its prevailing winds, regularly charting its high and low pressure area."

But he was just as keenly attuned to the air people breathed outside the literary world. He was motivated to move to New York in the early 1960s by a desire to migrate from Boston's backwater to Manhattan's intellectual sea. There he rode the cresting wave of what he saw as a Freudian Thanatos surrounding the political assassinations of the 1960s, particularly that of Martin Luther King, to which he adverted in the unrhymed "sonnet" in the series "April 8, 1968," originally published in the *New York Review of Books:*

> At this point of civilization, this point of the world,
> the only satisfactory companion we
> can imagine is death—this morning, skin lumping in my
>   throat,
> I lie here, heavily breathing, the soul of New York.

His style may already have become too inaccessible by 1968, however, to be entirely convincing as the expression of his attempt to speak for America, as Whitman had done, in his own voice. For the height of that identification one must turn to his best book, *Life Studies,* and "Memories of West Street and Lepke." The poem begins with a self-portrait of conspicuous consumption and lassitude: "I hog a whole house on Boston's / 'hardly passionate Marlborough Street' "—the quotation from William James serving both to sketch in the upper-middle-class setting and to provide historical continuity with Lowell's Victorian ancestors. In his *Robert Lowell: Life and Art,* Steven

Gould Axelrod comments: "This quoted phrase has been credited to Henry James by some commentators, but the actual source is William James, who once gave his classes the sentence, 'Marlborough is hardly a passionate street' as an example of understatement."

Yet wasteful and luxurious living know no class boundaries in 1950s America, the poem satirically suggests, for "even the man / scavenging filth in the back alley trash cans, / has two children, a beach wagon, a helpmate, / and is a 'young Republican.' " Behind the satire lurks the *Partisan Review* intellectual's fury at the lack of proletarian consciousness among the American lower classes.

Lowell's brilliance as a coiner of resonant phrases Madison Avenue could envy explodes into the poem with the line-and-a-half I have already quoted: "These are the tranquillized *Fifties*, / and I am forty." The man and his times are, in that phrase, at the same time yoked and out of step. Other poems from *Life Studies* tell us that Lowell, recovering from a mental breakdown, is himself literally tranquilized. "Cured," he states in "Home after Three Months Away," "I am frizzled, stale and small." In this chastened condition the poet can deprecate his letter of refusal to Roosevelt as a "manic statement, / telling off the state and president"; but behind the self-mockery a sense of shame chafes at his conscience.

Having engaged himself passionately with, taken pleasure and suffered at the hands of several of society's institutions—marriage, family, school, church, mental hospital, government—Lowell is our most subversive and incisive critic of these institutions. "In a central way, Robert Lowell was not quite civilized," Frank Bidart has written, and from his shaggy, renegade vantage point Lowell tended, sometimes in the most shocking way, to view our institutions in terms of one another, as though they were almost interchangeable. He sees the roof of the West Street Jail, where he served a year as a C.O. during World War II, as "a short / enclosure like my school soccer court." Later in the poem the jail metamorphoses, almost imperceptibly, into a microcosm of what Lowell and other intellectuals thought about American society during the Cold War. A "fellow jailbird" acts as the poet's informant about life in this microcosm, and particularly about the Mafia executioner Lepke:

> He taught me the "hospital tuck,"
> and pointed out the T-shirted back
> of *Murder Incorporated's* Czar Lepke,
> there piling towels on a rack,
> or dawdling off to his little segregated cell full
> of things forbidden the common man:
> a portable radio, a dresser, two toy American
> flags tied together with a ribbon of Easter palm.
> Flabby, bald, lobotomized,
> he drifted in a sheepish calm,
> where no agonizing reappraisal
> jarred his concentration on the electric chair—
> hanging like an oasis in his air
> of lost connections.

Received opinion about this period in American poetry has it that in *Life Studies* Lowell abandoned the formal style of his early work for "free verse." We would do well, however, to ponder T. S. Eliot's assertion that "there is no freedom in art," and—in writing about Ezra Pound—that "no verse is free for the man who wants to do a good job." It is true that some of the *Life Studies* poems are simply prose passages from his notebook, broken down into lines—"My Last Afternoon with Uncle Devereux Winslow" is a good example of this technique.

But more interesting from a metrical point of view are poems like "Memories of West Street and Lepke," where rhymes occur irregularly and the rhythms are variations of iambic. Two lines that occur shortly before the passage I have quoted, "I was so out of things, I'd never heard / of the Jehovah's Witnesses," are iambics—the first a pentameter, the second a tetrameter—varied only by a trochaic reversal in the first foot of the first line: a standard variation that may be observed in every verse practitioner from Shakespeare to James Merrill.

The partial rhymes, as well, are such as can be seen in the verse of Thomas Hardy, Wilfred Owen, W. H. Auden, Seamus Heaney. The rhymes' sense of random jaggedness—*tuck/back/*

rack, with *Lepke,* even, weirdly echoing those same rhymes—goes very well with the scene, which to allude to the title of Lowell's first collection, is a "land of unlikeness." John Foster Dulles, in the wake of increased tension between the United States and the Soviet Union, had promised an "agonizing reappraisal" of our foreign policy; the implied similitude between the electric chair and an impending nuclear war was clear to readers in the 1950s. With his command of traditional meters, Lowell raises the poem's energy to a suggestion of grand closure with the fully rhymed couplet,

> jarred his concentration on the electric chair—
> hanging like an oasis in his air

then undercuts it with the unrhymed, disoriented last line, "of lost connections."

Lowell has made Lepke into an image of postwar America as seen by a social critic of the left. Like America before *Brown v. Board of Education,* Lepke inhabits a "segregated cell," where he practices a kind of consumerism "forbidden the common man." Having tied "two toy American flags" together with "a ribbon of Easter palm," he affirms the unconstitutional alliance between Church and State. In the coziness of his domestic arrangements Lepke seems the epitome of Hannah Arendt's "banality of evil."

What is clear in retrospect, which I am not sure was clear at the time, is the resemblance between Lepke, America, and Robert Lowell himself. Recovering from treatment for a severe manic attack, Lowell sees himself as "Flabby, bald, lobotomized" (not surgically, but chemically) and "sheepish." Lowell's political criticism had, in Aristotelian terms, the defects of its qualities. As long as one could imagine the government being blindly violent and overbearing, as Lowell was in his manic phases, and then directionless and apologetic, as he was in the subsequent depressive periods of recuperation, Lowell was the ideal Everyman to portray the State of the Union.

During the years of the heady 1960s it was possible to credit Robert Lowell's portraits of tryants and other powerful men, informed and energized by his own fascination with power. An irony of Lowell's satirical portrait of Lyndon Johnson is that the poet enjoyed dominating a conversation among friends just as much as the president enjoyed dominating his staff. The driven poet, thoroughly in command in the world of letters, setting new literary trends, redefining the rules of the game, saw something of the dictator in himself:

> Stalin? What shot him clawing up the tree of power—
> millions plowed under like the crops they grew,
> his intimates dying like the spider-bridegroom?
> The large stomach could only chew success. What raised him
> was the usual lust to break the icon,
> joke cruelly, seriously, and be himself.
>
> "Stalin," *Notebook 1967–68*

How strong Lowell's own iconoclasm was, how reminiscent that the last line is of his own manner of joking! Dudley Young, described in Jeffrey Meyers's collection, *Robert Lowell: Interviews and Memoirs,* as "Lowell's sometime colleague, housemate and manservant at Essex University during 1970–71," gets the tone of Lowell's company during one of his "up" periods just right: "that voluminous brain, the relentless talk, the charm, the wit, the malice: all driven by a deceptively powerful body burning manic energy and whisky at about twice the rate of us who were half his age. He was the large and lethal Carnival King, the Candlemas Bear come to release us from common prose; sublime, sexy, and frequently mad."

But the figure that truly clicked with the poet's own fantasy was the king who was also an outlaw. Lowell's favorite brand of lawlessness and transcendence was sexual—"All life's grandeur is something with a girl in summer," he proclaimed in "Waking Early Sunday Morning." "What raised him" is of course a phallic pun. Writing in *Notebook 1967–68* about the capture and killing of Che Guevara, he explicitly identifies his own transgressions with those of the guerilla leader:

> Manhattan, where our clasped, illicit hands
> pulse, stop the bloodstream as if it hit rock. . . .
> Rest for the outlaw . . . kings once hid in oaks,
> with prices on their heads, and watched for game.

Such was the intricacy of Lowell's imaginative grappling with the fate of our nation in those years when the world seemed to come unglued, social barriers were breached, and idealism and barbarism shared the national stage. I am not suggesting that Robert Lowell exemplified the era—even at the time, with his patrician appearance and manner, he struck observers as anachronistic, "elitist," off-center. But he rose to the challenge of stamping his imprint on the times and was honored for having done so. Norman Mailer in *Armies of the Night* nicely suggests the way Lowell captivated the antiwar crowd by not *trying* to captivate them:

> Still, he made no effort to win the audience, seduce them, dominate them, bully them, amuse them, no, they were there for him, to please *him*, a sounding board for the plucked string of his poetic line, and so he endeared himself to them. They adored him—for his talent, his modesty, his superiority, his melancholy, his petulance, his weakness, his painful, almost stammering shyness, his noble strength—*there* was the string behind other strings.

Perhaps inevitably a literary reputation declines after an author's death. Yet Lowell's reputation seems to have hit harder times than his contemporaries could have predicted. Why has this happened? Lowell's life and art were famously, dangerously, one. I'll focus on two trends that make our age a chilly one for a man who, as poet and person, imposed himself so mightily on his own age. The first of these is a misreading of Lowell the man. Ian Hamilton's 1982 biography (see "Damaged Grandeur" in this volume) left an impression of turmoil and scandal, breakdown on the heels of breakdown.

Hamilton knew Lowell only in his later years, during his residence in England, and never knew him well. Because the man's excesses and hospitalizations are easier to document than his private kindnesses, his table talk, his warmth and loyalty to friends, the biography is more case study than life study. Lowell unfortunately had no Boswell to record his conversation, which is a great pity. Still, the power of his magnetism is evidenced by the plenitude of brief memoirs that do exist (most of them collected in Meyers). His friend, the ballet dancer Esther Brooks, wrote one of the best. "When someone says Robert Lowell to me, or Cal, as he was known to his friends," she begins,

> an instantaneous picture comes to mind: Cal sitting in a chair, his head inclined a bit to one side, his chin pressed slightly down, his magnified eyes peering through their lenses at you, one hand holding a drink, the other raised in front of his chest, palm out jabbing at the air, a cigarette between the index and middle finger, dropping ashes all over his shirt front, talking and talking and commanding your whole attention. The only variation is the expression on his face. Depending on my own mood, I suppose, I can see him looking introspective and intense; at other times, choking back his merriment, his lower lip becoming thicker with some impending verbal mischief, or again a look of anguish brought on by some thought of doom, of man's fate, or of the world gone so madly awry.

In her review of the Hamilton biography Helen Vendler lamented the lack of an *intellectual* biography, since Lowell as a thinker is surely more interesting than as a mental case. Esther Brooks captures some sense of the variety, scope, and intensity of his conversation:

> When Cal was well he was enormous fun to be with. His way of looking at things was so completely original that you yourself began to see everything from a different perspective. Hours meant nothing to him when he was interested. Day turned into night and night back into day while he, with his seemingly limitless stamina, worried an idea, rejected it, discovered another, built mental pyramids, tore them down, discoursed on the habits of wolves, the Punic Wars, Dante, Napoleon, Shakespeare, Alexander the Great, politics, his friends, religion, his work, or the great noyade at Nantes. Whatever the subject it all came forth as though it were being pushed at you, helped on its way by that outward prodding palm. Sometimes this incredible energy of his would exhaust you and you would suddenly feel like screaming, or running away in search of some undefined moment, some unexamined fact, some purely sensuous reaction to beauty.

Lowell is famous for having written, "I am tired, everyone's tired of my turmoil." But the word I recall his using more characteristically is not "turmoil" but "joy." A conversation, a visit, a meeting with friends was "a joy." A concordance to the poetry would surely find many instances of the word, including this one from "Plane-Ticket," a late "sonnet":

> After fifty so much joy has come,
> I hardly want to hide my nakedness—
> the shine and stiffness of a new suit, a feeling,
> not wholly happy, of having been reborn.

Readers, particularly readers of a certain age, with any experience of the tea-and-crumpets "Poetry Society" scene as it existed in this country until about twenty-five years ago, will be able to appreciate how crucial was the encouragement Robert Lowell gave to female students such as Anne Sexton and Sylvia Plath—the encouragement to break away from the cloyingly genteel, "lady poet" milieu of the times. It is to this milieu and its stereotypes that Lowell was referring in his preface to the American edition of Sylvia Plath's *Ariel:* "In these poems, written in the last months of her life and often rushed out at the rate of two or three a day, Sylvia Plath becomes herself, becomes something imaginary, newly, wildly, and subtly created—hardly a person at all, or a woman, certainly not another 'poetess,' but one of those super-real, hypnotic, great classical heroines. This character is feminine, rather than female, though almost everything we customarily think of as feminine is turned on its head."

Among the grave and at the same time comic consequences of poetry's current sequestration in universities is that academic critics are now able to set the standards by which poets are judged. Harold Bloom, whose writings enjoyed an academic vogue as recently as a decade ago, has argued for the exclusion of Robert Lowell's poetry from the canon, expressing "the conviction that Robert Lowell is anything but a permanent poet, that he has been mostly a maker of period-pieces from his origins until now." Bloom is author of *The Anxiety of*

Influence as well as some hundred other titles, including *A Map of Misreading*, dedicated to Paul de Man and purporting to offer "instruction in the practical criticism of poetry, in how to read a poem." The self-aggrandizement of the critic as "strong reader" is obvious: "what I myself would call a new mythic being—clearly implied by Paul de Man in particular— the reader as Overman, the *Überleser*. This fictive reader . . . at once blind and transparent with light, self-deconstructed yet fully knowing the pain of his separation both from text and nature, doubtless will be more than equal to the revisionary labors of contraction and destruction."

Central to Bloom's understanding of poetry is the notion of "influence," whereby the "strong" poet harbors oedipal resentments against his "strong precursors" ("strong" is a favorite Bloomian adjective), whom he strives to displace. "Influence, as I conceive it, means that there are *no* texts, but only relationships *between* texts": an assertion that for understandable reasons has been greeted with incredulity by writers, and by readers who have little interest in contemporary critical theory. In the days of the New Criticism, which is currently in bad odor in the academy, critics understood their task to be one of commenting on poems, stories, novels, in a way that would assist readers. If in that sense we understand the poet or novelist to be the father of the critic, Bloom has clearly attempted a Freudian coup of his own, supplanting the poet with the critic, because in his mind it is not the poem but the "critical act" that takes center stage:

> These relationships [between "texts"] depend upon a critical act, a misreading or misprision, that one poet performs upon another, and that does not differ in kind from the necessary critical acts performed by every strong reader upon every text he encounters. The influence-relation governs reading as it governs writing, and reading is therefore a miswriting just as writing is a misreading. As literary history lengthens, all poetry necessarily becomes verse-criticism, just as all criticism becomes prose-poetry.

That Bloom can view his own criticism—with its obfuscation and arcane private vocabulary, transparent only in its ambition to replace the poet with the critic—as "prose-poetry" would be enough to call into question his literary taste. What one would like to understand is why he has attacked Lowell so roundly. The reason seems to be that he cannot find a place for Lowell in a line of philosphically minded American poets with roots in Emerson, descending from Wallace Stevens down to the contemporary poets A. R. Ammons and John Ashbery.

Clearly it bothers Bloom that Lowell, like Elizabeth Bishop, has such a strong allegiance to "what really happened." Yet despite—or perhaps even because of—his imperiled purchase on quotidian reality, Lowell belongs to the line of American poets who assert, with William Carlos Williams, that

> so much depends
> upon
>
> a red wheel
> barrow
>
> glazed with rain
> water
>
> beside the white
> chickens

and who relish Robert Frost's brisk physicality in lines like these about chopping wood, from "Two Tramps in Mud Time":

> Good blocks of beech it was I split,
> As large around as the chopping block;
> And every piece I squarely hit
> Fell splinterless as a cloven rock.

As Seamus Heaney has said of his first encounters with the poetry of Patrick Kavanagh, "What was being experienced was not some hygienic and self-aware pleasure of the text but a primitive delight in finding the world become word." That we cherish poetry's enhancement of the world in which we live does not sit well with Harold Bloom, who insists that poetry must be hermetic and self-referential:

> Every poem we know begins as an encounter *between poems*. I am aware that poets and their readers prefer to believe otherwise, but acts, persons, and places, if they are to be handled by poems at all, must themselves be treated first as though they were already poems, or parts of poems. Contact, in a poem, means contact with another poem, even if that poem is called a deed, person, place or thing.

How sad this attitude is, full of the tedium of footnotes and card catalogues! The reason those who care about poetry should vigorously confront and reject it is that what it wishes for poetry is nothing less than death.

Despite the shifting winds of critical fashion, Lowell remains the greatest American poet of the midcentury. One need not draw invidious comparisons with other poets to make this claim. The immense variety of our poetry is part of its appeal. But no one has filled—no one has had the ambition to fill— the void left by Lowell's death. Part of what made him, in his time, a poet whom everyone felt compelled to read was his seriousness. The camp, "put on," pastiche, or parody approaches associated with postmodernism represent a reaction against seriousness in the arts; one can see how out of fashion this aesthetic makes Lowell seem. Aside from Donald Hall— himself hardly fashionable among postmodernists—it is hard to imagine one of our contemporaries elegizing what was best about American tradition as Lowell did in "For the Union Dead":

> On a thousand small town New England greens,
> the old white churches hold their air
> of sparse, sincere rebellion; frayed flags
> quilt the graveyards of the Grand Army of the Republic.

And is there a social critic among today's poets with the vision and intellectual depth to found his critique of our society on history and on the predatory instincts tragically inherent in human nature? Having earlier in the poem celebrated Col. Robert Gould Shaw and his black regiment, the Massachusetts 54th, with the Latin epigraph, *"Relinquunt Omnia Servare Rem Publicam"* (They gave up everything to serve the state), Lowell indelibly pictures the contemporary degradation of the ideal of public service:

> Everywhere,
> giant finned cars nose forward like fish;
> a savage servility
> slides by on grease.

Though he often acknowledged his own solipsism and bookish isolation from the world of power, he was never so foolish as to deny that world's reality, or to suppose that poetry could not touch that world. It would be the greatest of pleasures to hear him take off on the notion that "acts, persons, and places, if they are to be handled by poems at all, must themselves be treated first as though they were already poems."

What makes him indispensable, whether one shares his political positions or not, is his knowledge that, no matter what the latest intellectual fashion emanating from Paris says, money still talks, political power still comes from the barrel of a gun, human nature is still capable of appalling atrocities, and the writer still has a role to play as witness and critic. When we lost Lowell we lost a voice of conscience, someone who could cast his acts of witness into resonant phrases we could not avoid listening to. Lowell agreed with Aristotle that art is mimesis, an imitation of reality, and with Matthew Arnold that poetry is a criticism of life. In an intellectual climate so eager to see "the death of the author," one can appreciate how disturbing the continuing presence of a poet like Lowell must be.

Damaged Grandeur
The Life of Robert Lowell

When *Life Studies* appeared in 1959, John Thompson wrote in the *Kenyon Review* that "the great past, Revolutionary America, the Renaissance, Rome, is all contemporary to [Lowell]. He moves among its great figures at ease with his peers. . . . This is why, perhaps alone of living poets, he can bear for us the role of the great poet, the man who on a very large scale sees more, feels more, and speaks more bravely about it than we ourselves can do." Earlier in Lowell's career Peter Viereck had judged him "best qualified to restore to our literature its sense of the tragic and the lofty."

Largeness of scale was part of Lowell's makeup. He came into the world with a sense of grandeur:

> I too was born under the shadow of the Dome of the Boston State House and under Pisces, the Fish, on the first of March 1917. America was entering the First World War and was about to play her part in the downfall of four empires.

Thus begins an unfinished autobiographical piece, unpublished during his lifetime, which appeared in his posthumously published *Collected Prose* under the title "Antebellum Boston." The two sentences I have quoted wonderfully capture Lowell's essence. If the dramatic self-proclamation seems presumptuous—well, the phenomenon of Robert Lowell really was awe-inspiring. The juxtaposition of the personal with a crucial historical moment became a trademark of his poetry.

Lowell has, as a historical poet, few rivals among modern

writers. Few poets have the erudition (not to speak of the brazenness) to link their birth with a world war and the decline of the British, German, Hapsburg, and Czarist Russian empires. But Lowell's preoccupation with historical turning points was characteristic. His manic-depressive mental illness (bipolar disorder) expressed itself in flights of enthusiasm, which took the form of highly excited identifications with powerful figures from history such as Napoleon, Alexander the Great, Churchill, Stalin, Hitler. This tendency began in childhood:

> And I, bristling and manic,
> skulked in the attic,
> and got two hundred French generals by name,
> From *A* to *V*—from Augereau to Vandamme.
> I used to dope myself asleep,
> naming those unpronounceables like sheep.
>
> "Commander Lowell"

An obsession with Napoleon runs through Lowell's madness, an enthusiasm he shared, or so he claims in "Antebellum Boston," with his mother when she was a girl: "She began to bolt her food, and for a time slept on an Army cot and took cold dips in the morning. In all this she could be Napoleon made over in my grandfather's Prussian image. It was always my grandfather she admired, even if she called him Napoleon." Napoleon as a pint-sized image of domination. "Mother, her strong chin unprotected and chilled in the helpless autumn, seemed to me the young Alexander, all gleam and panache. . . . Mother, also, was a sort of commander in chief of her virgin battlefield." Alexander was another of Lowell's favorite tyrants; Robert Silvers, quoted by Ian Hamilton, recalls that "at Mt. Sinai [hospital] he talked in a wandering way about Alexander the Great—how Philip of Macedon had been a canny politician but Alexander had been able to cut through Asia." His manic attacks were sometimes heralded by his wearing a medallion of Alexander the Great around his neck, or reading *Mein Kampf* (Jonathan Miller writes that Lowell kept a copy of it inside the dust jacket of Baudelaire's *Les Fleurs du mal*), or buying a bust of Napoleon and displaying it on his dining room table in his apartment on West 67th Street in New York.

If we are to come to a better understanding of Robert Lowell's life and art, we need first of all to examine some of the misconceptions engendered by what has until recently been the only biography of him available: Ian Hamilton's massive, handsomely turned out, but often misleading 1982 work. As with Lawrance Thompson's biography of Robert Frost, many readers—even if they have not read the book—have a sense of the poet they assume to be accurate. The Hamilton biography makes it easy—a bit too easy—to jump to conclusions about Lowell's megalomania. Even when the book was being written, what I learned of its preparation made me wonder whether Hamilton's methods might not be rather hasty and hit-or-miss. Since it was, for years, the only biography, I want to take a close look at it here.

Hamilton focuses on the more sensationalistic aspects of Lowell's public life rather than on the extraordinary life of the mind that gave the poetry its depth. In addition, the way he thanks Jason Epstein of Random House "for commissioning the book" suggests that he was hired to undertake the project rather than initiating it on his own. This makes one question his personal stake in the project—though, despite adopting a consistently snide and carping tone throughout the book, by the end even Hamilton becomes overwhelmed by the air of damaged grandeur associated with Lowell's life.

Hamilton has gone on to write a book about J. D. Salinger and another called *Writers in Hollywood,* and has edited *The Faber Book of Soccer.* It is unfortunate that the "definitive" biographer of Robert Lowell, the subtleties of whose poems are extremely hard to grasp outside the American context, should not be an American. As an Englishman, Hamilton simply lacks the ear to interpret, or misses the tone of, much of the material he is confronted with. A sensitivity to social nuance is essential to an understanding of much of Lowell's work, *Life Studies* above all. As one small instance of how lost Hamilton is in this most important area, he presents Lowell's grandfather Arthur Winslow as "a Boston boy who had made his middle-sized pile as a mining engineer in Colorado . . . almost ridiculously proud of his descent from the New England Winslows who had supported George III," as though Winslow were some sort of jumped-up, socially insecure *nouveau riche,* and not what he was: a typical son of a good Boston family. I've never heard the expression "a Boston boy" in my life.

If Sylvia Plath's *Ariel* was, as Lowell wrote in his introduction to the book, "the autobiography of a fever," Hamilton's biography of Lowell is the biography of a psychosis. But Lowell was, like Hamlet, "but mad north-north-west"; when the wind was southerly he too knew "a hawk from a handsaw." His attacks, and the subsequent recovery periods, typically lasted one to two months. My calculations indicate that Hamilton devotes, by a rough page-count, one-fourth of his account of Lowell's adult life to the poet's madness, thereby giving readers of the biography the impression that Lowell was off his rocker more than twice as much of the time as he actually was. Caroline Blackwood comments in a 1993 interview in *Town and Country,* "There was the mad Cal, but that was less than half the person—only a few months every year" (and even here, she is speaking of Lowell's last years, when the bouts of insanity came more frequently).

What astounded Lowell's friends was how quickly and substantially he was able to recover from his manic episodes: "In between," Blair Clark wrote in a letter quoted by Hamilton, "Cal functions brilliantly, and I mean this to apply not only to his writing but to his personal and family life." Writing in the 1986 collection, *Robert Lowell: Essays on the Poetry,* which he also edited, Steven Gould Axelrod endeavors to explain why Hamilton's book has left readers with the sense that having read it, they know what there is to know about Robert Lowell:

> First, of course, Hamilton's ability to persuade Lowell's intimates and executors to help him has seemed to give his book an official imprimatur. Second, Hamilton does indeed reveal more information about Lowell's private life, especially its scandalous side. . . . But I believe another factor has played a crucial role in the book's success. Hamilton's genius is in relating the most sordid personal details in a tone of effortless, agree-

able superiority. Reading *Robert Lowell: A Biography* is like reading the *National Enquirer* firm in the conviction that one is actually perusing the *Times Literary Supplement.*

Lowell's second wife, Elizabeth Hardwick, who was in the best, or worst, position to speak of his attacks and recoveries is quoted by Hamilton as saying that

> it seemed so miraculous that the old gifts of person and art were still there, as if they had been stored in some serene, safe box somewhere. Then it did not seem possible that the dread assault could return to hammer him into bits once more.
>
> He "came to" sad, worried, always ashamed and fearful; and yet there he was, this unique soul for whom one felt great pity. . . . Out of the hospital, he returned to his days, which were regular, getting up early in the morning, going to his room or separate place for work. All day long he lay on the bed, propped up on an elbow. And this was his life, reading, studying and writing. The papers piled up on the floor, the books on the bed, the bottles of milk on the window sill, and the ashtray filled. . . . The discipline, the dedication, the endless adding to his *store,* by reading and studying—all this had, in my view, much that was heroic about it.

To reverse the terms of the old Aristotelian chestnut, Lowell had the qualities of his defects. He had not only that sense of self-assurance without which it is hard to see how anyone writes poetry at all, but also the luck to have been born with a name and family tradition that lent authority to his utterances. Elizabeth Bishop was keenly aware of the many advantages life had dropped in Lowell's lap—advantages that had been denied her. When she remarks, in the letter to Lowell I quoted in the Introduction, "In some ways you are the luckiest poet I know!," the first three words of her sentence are weighty ones. This luckiest of all our poets turned out to be one of the unluckiest. Both as poet and man, Lowell presents an awesome spectacle of great gifts, great luck, and great misfortune. This tragic imbalance is what gives his story overtones of classical heroism.

The young Lowell was notorious for his single-mindedness,

ambition, lack of humor, and belief in aristocratic ideals. "I am not flattered by the remark that you do not know where I am heading or that my ways are not your ways," he wrote at age twenty-three to his tyrannical mother: "I am heading exactly where I have been heading for six years. One can hardly be ostracized for taking the intellect and aristocracy and family tradition seriously." As a teenager, he had prescribed for his friends not only a reading and self-improvement program, but even, during a summer on Nantucket with two schoolmates, the daily menu: "We had dreadful health food all the time. The diet was eels—cooked by me, badly—and a dreadful cereal with raw honey. All decided by Cal."

Lord Weary's Castle, Lowell's first major collection, can be seen as a proud, forbidding citadel that the poet erected around himself. The title was already a good indication that here was a poet who would concern himself with the exercise of power, both on the personal and political levels. Robert Hass, in the essay "Lowell's Graveyard" from *Twentieth Century Pleasures,* writes:

> "The Quaker Graveyard" is not a political poem. I had assumed that it was, that its rage against the war and Puritan will and the Quakers of Nantucket who financed the butchery of whales was an attack on American capitalism. But a political criticism of any social order implies both that a saner one can be imagined and the hope or conviction that it can be achieved. . . . I went back to the poem looking for the vision of an alternative world. There is none.

If optimism about alternative political solutions is a *sine qua non* of political poetry, then it must be concluded that Lowell was never a political poet at all. But I would have to disagree with Hass's strictures on political poetry. While remaining pessimistic about change, Lowell constantly engaged himself with the world of politics and power. His view of the radical alternatives to capitalism was just as dark as his critique of capitalism itself.

Received opinion has it Lowell started writing "personal" poetry only with *Life Studies,* a view that Robert Hass counters brilliantly in his essay:

I still find myself blinking incredulously when I read—in almost anything written about the poetry—that those early poems "clearly reflect the dictates of the new criticism," while the later ones are "less consciously wrought and extremely intimate." This is the view in which it is "more intimate" and "less conscious" to say "my mind's not right" than to imagine the moment when

> The death-lance churns into the sanctuary, tears
> The gun-blue swingle, heaving like a flail,
> And hacks the coiling life out . . .

which is to get things appallingly wrong.

Lowell's manner in "The Quaker Graveyard at Nantucket" is to manhandle the iambic pentameter with strong spondees and enjambments learned from Milton, and to express an extreme mental derangement through violent imagery and logical absurdities. Speaking of the lines "Where the heelheaded dogfish barks its nose / On Ahab's void and forehead," Hass comments, "The lines depend on our willingness to let barking dogs marry scavenging sharks in the deep places where men void and are voided. To complain about this is not to launch an attack on 'consciously wrought' but the reverse." So much for the fiction that in *Life Studies,* Lowell conformed to a culture-wide shift from the cooked to the raw, from paleface to redskin, though he himself publicly made the case for such a view. For poets like Galway Kinnell, Robert Bly, and Adrienne Rich, free verse really did mean what the name implies. For Lowell, what are misleadingly called fixed forms meant freedom and madness, while free verse meant prose, sanity, and control.

In the deepest part of his psyche, Lowell was, I suspect, that tyrant, that pure id that always longed to "break loose," to dominate, to be the entire world. Writing "imitations" of poets from Homer to Pasternak, for example, he "Lowellized" (Hamilton's term) his originals, making their poems sound like his own. There was not a drop of Wordsworthian "wise passivity" in his veins. In a poem written later in life, he addressed a bit of light but telling raillery to his wife and daughter: "I hope, of course, you both will outlive me, / but you and

Harriet are perhaps like countries / not yet ripe for self-determination." (Alan Williamson, in a letter to me dated 5 December 1993, reports Lowell's claim that the words here were Elizabeth Hardwick's, not his, which puts the matter in quite a different light.)

In person he could shamelessly bully the weak and even the strong, often charmingly. But the tyrant shared a bed with the rebel, as Lowell himself understood. His sense of humor—and Hamilton gives little sense of it—was mischievously subversive. In "Grandparents," written when he inherited his grandfather's summer place, he grieves for his grandfather, who is "Never again to walk there, chalk our cues, / insist on shooting for us both," but concludes with: "I hold an *Illustrated London News*—; / disloyal still, / I doodle handle-bar / mustaches on the last Russian Czar." Being both dictator and revolutionary allowed him a unique view of politics. Given the contradictions inherent in this position, naturally he was a pessimist. Prometheus, in Lowell's "Prometheus Bound," sums up the position: "It is impossible to think too much about power."

Lowell as a political poet remains, for all his brilliance and insight, something of a creature of the 1960s, along with the Kennedys, Eugene McCarthy, Che Guevara, and Lyndon Johnson, all of whom appear in his poems. Pronouncements on America from those years have a way of sounding, in retrospect, excitedly and unjustifiably apocalyptic. Hamilton's evaluation is sound: "His difficulty was that his image of America was not too sharply different from his image of himself." On the other hand, it was Lowell's own violent nature, perhaps, that made him healthily skeptical of the glibness with which many of us promoted a potentially violent revolution during that giddy decade. If James Atlas's "Robert Lowell in Cambridge: Lord Weary" is accurate, Lowell's comments on former students who, like me—fictionalized as "Leonard Wiggins"— had been swept up in left-wing politics, were rather caustic but not unfair:

> "What about Leonard Wiggins?" I said. He had gone out to California for the semester and "been through a lot of heavy changes," he reported in a letter I now quoted to Lowell.

"Yes, I gather he's brimming with revolutionary zeal," Lowell said, leaning forward to concentrate on my words. (What a keen pleasure that was!) He loved news of anyone he knew. "I like his early poems, but I can't follow what he's writing now. You wonder if there isn't too much California in it." (He always switched from "I" to "you," as if attributing his opinions to someone else.)

The side of Lowell's personality that needed to dominate was balanced by a side that liked to be led. Writing about his acrimonious home life with his parents, John Crowe Ransom (quoted in Steven Gould Axelrod's *Robert Lowell: Life and Art*) calls it "a bad hurt for a boy who would have revered all his elders if they were not unworthy." In the 1940s both Ransom and Allen Tate were to some degree surrogate fathers to Lowell, though Tate winced at being called "Father Tate." And Randall Jarrell, Lowell's elder by only three years—Lowell's pet name for him was "the Old Man"—always, though a lifelong close friend, remained a distant and austere critic of Lowell's poetry.

His relationship with Jarrell, who had the surest taste in poetry of anyone in his generation, is another example of Lowell's wonderful luck. An even more important bit of luck was his marriage to Elizabeth Hardwick. Hardwick's acerbic wit, in conversation and in print, is famous if not notorious. The tintype saint from Hamilton's book is an image that few of her friends would recognize. She married, took care of, and tolerated all manner of outrageous behavior from a man who could be impossible. Part of what made Hardwick stick with him must have been love and family loyalty; part must have been a dedication to literature. Jarrell expressed what many people thought: "You feel before reading any new poem of his the uneasy expectation of perhaps encountering a masterpiece." It's clear that Lowell needed something like Hardwick's astringency to keep his native wildness under control: "your old-fashioned tirade— / loving, rapid, merciless— / breaks like the Atlantic Ocean on my head." He had also loved the gift his first wife, Jean Stafford, had for malicious gossip and slander. "Calumny!" he would shout delightedly. "Here comes the black tongue!" Readers with a Freudian inclination will not be surprised to learn that Lowell's mother also had a wickedly sharp tongue.

It was inevitable that Lowell would bite the hand that fed him. "O to break loose!" the opening of "Waking Early Sunday Morning," could have been his motto. After he left Hardwick, he wrote her: "What shall I say? That I miss your old guiding and even chiding hand. Not having you is like learning to walk. I suppose though one thing worse than stumbling and vacillating, is to depend on someone who does these things." Yet the sense of "breaking loose" that accompanied Lowell's estrangement from Elizabeth Hardwick and his move to England eventually brought personal unhappiness and confusion rather than clarity. His third marriage, to Caroline Blackwood, turned into a disaster—though not all of Lowell's friends would agree with my assessment. A friend writes:

> True, Caroline didn't have the stamina to deal with Cal's breakdowns, whereas Lizzie did. But, according to [mutual friends], the marriage with Lizzie had gotten so combative by 1970 as to be really unpleasant to be around. And there was something touching in Cal's sexual and protective affection for Caroline, and the way their slapdash, improvisatory approach to life made them good companions for each other, for a while.

On the fourteen-line poems (it is not accurate to refer to them as sonnets) he began writing in 1967 for *Notebook* and continued writing through 1973, which constitute *History, For Lizzie and Harriet,* and *The Dolphin,* I am inclined to agree with Ian Hamilton:

> The death of Randall Jarrell had removed the one critical voice that Lowell was in fear of—What will Randall think of *this?* had always been one of his first worries. It is possible that Jarrell might have found most of these new fourteen-liners slack, near-journalistic, or too much like casual diary jottings; they might have seemed to him too mumblingly unrhetorical, too self-indulgent. This is guessing; but there *is* a sense in which

Lowell's new surge of eloquence is also a surge of truancy from the idea of some absolute critical authority, a "breaking loose" from the requirement *never* to write badly.

Part of what is wrong with the fourteen-liners is a formal problem. Lowell's willfulness led him to think that if he could convince himself of the truth of something, then that was all that needed to be done. The fourteen-liners were little molds into which he could pour whatever he wished. The mere fact that they *resembled* sonnets was enough to make them do what sonnets have traditionally done in English poetry. In an After-thought to *Notebook 1967–68,* he avers, "My meter, fourteen line unrhymed blank verse sections, is fairly strict at first and elsewhere, but often corrupts in single lines to the freedom of prose. Even with this license, I fear I have failed to avoid the themes and gigantism of the sonnet." He was guarding the wrong flank: the poems need more, not less, of the traditional virtues (which he derides as "gigantism") of the sonnet se-quence. The gigantism came not from his approximation of the sonnet form, but from his own megalomania.

"Those blessed structures, plot and rhyme— / why are they no help to me now / I want to make / something imagined, not recalled?" Lowell asks in his last book, *Day by Day.* Perhaps they *would* have been a help to him, if he had had the disci-pline and deliberation to return to them. Hamilton identifies another problem of the "sonnets," one of tone: "there is some-thing glazed and foreign in their manner of address, as if they sense an audience too far-off, too blurred to be worth striving for." Lowell at his best is a very grounded, personal writer, and his prefatory remark to *Notebook 1967–68,* "Accident threw up subjects, and the plot swallowed them—famished for human chances," suggests an impersonality far from his genius. *Notebook* and its later incarnations have been seen by some critics as attempts to rival John Berryman's *Dream Songs.* If this was the case, Lowell might have done well to emulate the *Dream Songs'* formal division into stanzas.

Furious debate surrounded the ethics of Lowell's having included the letters, telephone conversations, and so on of Elizabeth Hardwick in his late books, *The Dolphin* and *For*

Lizzie and Harriet. His friend William Alfred was strongly against it. W. H. Auden said he would never speak to Lowell again if he published the Hardwick material. Elizabeth Bishop wrote him an impassioned letter trying to dissuade him from publishing an earlier version of *The Dolphin:*

> That is "infinite mischief," I think. The first one, page 10, is so shocking—well, I don't know what to say. . . . One can use one's life as material—one does, anyway—but these letters— aren't you violating a trust? IF you were given permission—IF you hadn't changed them . . . etc. *But art just isn't worth that much.* . . . It is not being "gentle" to use personal, tragic, anguished letters that way—it's cruel.

To Lowell, though, life and art were one. His loyalties were, finally, to his work.

But in his last book, *Day by Day,* Lowell seems to say that he has botched not only his life, but his poetry as well. Perhaps he was writing his own epitaph when he addressed these words to his namesake: "yours the lawlessness / of something simple that has lost its law, / my namesake, not the last Caligula." He could perhaps have endured the pain of inflicting pain on his family. In fact, in the last poem of *The Dolphin* he shoulders that responsibility:

> I have sat and listened to too many
> words of the collaborating muse,
> and plotted perhaps too freely with my life,
> not avoiding injury to others,
> not avoiding injury to myself—
> to ask compassion . . . this book, half fiction,
> an eelnet made by man for the eel fighting—
>
> my eyes have seen what my hand did.
>
> "Dolphin"

Writing in the *American Poetry Review* in 1973, Adrienne Rich delivered the strongest condemnation of the three books of "sonnets." Harsh as her words are, it is hard to disagree with Rich's assessment of the lines from *The Dolphin,* except that what she sees as vindictiveness is more truly a colossal thoughtlessness:

> I have to say that I think this is bullshit eloquence, a poor excuse for a cruel and shallow book, that it is presumptuous to balance injury done to others with injury done to myself—and that the question remains, after all—to what purpose? The inclusion of the letter poems stands as one of the most vindictive and mean-spirited acts in the history of poetry, one for which I can think of no precedent: and the same unproportioned ego that was capable of this act is damagingly at work in all three of Lowell's books.

Lowell was not completely written out when he died at sixty. The poems in *Day by Day* demonstrate that he had abandoned the crutch the fourteen-line form had become for him during the period of *History;* the anguished candor of the new poems suggests that, had he lived, he might have achieved another poetic breakthrough as important as the one he brought off in *Life Studies.* Sixty might, in some people, seem a ripe enough age to die. Not for Lowell, of whom one can say that he "should have died hereafter." In the meantime Paul Mariani's new biography of Lowell gives readers a more rounded picture of the "Cal" his friends put up with, laughed about, became exasperated with, but always admired and deeply loved.

To say that his friends laughed about him may sound cruel; but sad as his life in some ways was, why not grant the man credit for being one in a long line of aristocratic Boston eccentrics? Ian Hamilton quotes Keith Botsford, who accompanied Lowell on a Congress for Cultural Freedom junket to South America. Botsford would visit Lowell in the hospital in Buenos Aires during one of his attacks and recalls:

> I was brought up as a composer, and all he wanted me to do was whistle. Sometimes it was "Yankee Doodle Dandy" or "The Battle Hymn of the Republic." Or it was Brandenberg concertos, Mozart piano concertos, anything. It was the one thing he craved, the one thing that would calm him. I'd be there two or

three hours, just whistling until I was dry in the mouth. I'd whistle all the parts in the Ninth Symphony, or whatever, and he'd say, "Yeah, but do the tympani bit."

I leave the last word to Peter Taylor, one of Lowell's oldest friends, in his funeral oration:

As poet, as man, he approaches the great mystery playfully and seriously at the same time. From the very beginning or from the time when I first knew him in his later teens, he seemed determined that there should be no split in his approach to understanding profound matters. He was searching for a one-ness in himself and a oneness in the world. He would not allow that any single kind of experience denied him the right and access to some opposite kind. . . . He would boast at times that he had never lost a friend. He never even wanted to give up a marriage entirely. He wanted his wife and children around him in an old fashioned household, and yet he wanted to be free and on the town. Who *doesn't* wish for all that, of course? But he *would* have both. He wanted it all so intensely that he became very sick at times. . . . When one heard that he was dead and how he died in the back seat of a New York taxi cab, one could not help feeling that he had everything, even the kind of death he had always said he wanted.

Robert Lowell Midstream:
"What Next, What Next?"

In *Life Studies* (1959) Robert Lowell dramatized the life of a man who, although comfortably well-off, the descendant of a distinguished Boston family, admirably educated, and intellectually brilliant, suffered tragically from emotional upset, mental breakdown, and conflict with the political orthodoxies of his day. While detailing his childhood and social milieu, bringing his parents and grandparents vividly—often disturbingly—to life, Lowell also managed to put his dilemma into context by executing deft portraits of several contemporary literary figures, as well as characters from history. He demonstrated a command of literary architectonics that would put most writers to shame. At the same time, he achieved a readable style unlike that of any other poet. While taking advantage of the spontaneity and resourcefulness of free verse, his poems retain the resonance and memorability of rhyme and meter. *Life Studies* remains his highest achievement. Still, the discoveries to be made by looking before and after that achievement can be surprising and instructive. My focus here is *For the Union Dead,* first published in 1964.

In terms of raw genius, high animal spirits, fecundity of imagination, and command of the medium alone, Lowell may be said to have peaked even earlier, with the composition, in the mid-1940s, of "The Quaker Graveyard in Nantucket." The poem suffers, though, from being in places more or less incomprehensible, and its overall plan is shaky. One suspects that at first he found his own gift—a kind of pure energy that manipulated language at an almost preverbal, inchoate level—too bewildering and intimidating to control. Lowell in *Life Studies* reminds me a little of a pitcher, who, after losing the ability to throw the hard stuff, learns to win through guile and strategy. Throughout his life, people who knew the man remarked on his immense physical strength—particularly during his manic attacks, when he would have to be forcibly subdued—as well as his massive intellectual powers. He writes in "Waking Early Sunday Morning" of his "fierce, fireless mind, running downhill." Reading the entire *oeuvre*, one is haunted by the thought that this poet's entire career may be occurring on a declining curve.

Life Studies represented, in the eyes of its author, a compromise with the world, an accommodation. It is worth recalling that for Lowell, rhymed and metered poetry on the level of "The Quaker Graveyard," with its Miltonic grandeur and its habit of running roughshod over sense and logic, spoke for madness, while the prosy free verse of *Life Studies* spoke for sanity even while it dealt in madness. Writing of "the skirt-mad Mussolini" and his failed attempt to recreate the quasi-mythic synthesis of vision and power associated with the Classical world, Lowell in "Beyond the Alps" tellingly deflates Il Duce in these words: "He was one of us / only, pure prose." Though madness is ostensibly the subject of many of the *Life Studies* poems, it is madness viewed from the standpoint of the sane, or rather the cured: "I keep no rank or station. / Cured, I am frizzled, stale and small."

The *frisson* brought on by *Life Studies,* seen within its context as the most visible exemplum of the Confessional movement, came from its shocking openness. Readers were clearly thrilled by the experience—equal parts voyeurism, compassion, shock of recognition, and relief that their own lives were less extreme—of listening to raw confession. There were many things about the book that must have been exhilarating to its author: the sense of having made a clean breast of things, of discovering how poetry—even if part of him thought it poetry of a lower order—could be made of what was the main "stuff" of his experience. In addition, the book organizes itself around a symmetrical schema that makes it satisfyingly shapely.

Moving from *Life Studies* to *For the Union Dead*, which appeared in 1964, the problem, put simply, was how to follow it: "At forty-five," he asks in "Middle Age," one of the first poems in *For the Union Dead*, "what next, what next?" The citation of his exact age echoes the citation of his age in "Memories of West Street and Lepke." Though the book was roundly praised when it first appeared, it has tended to sit uneasily with later critics, who have found the transition from *Life Studies* perplexing and a falling off. Steven Gould Axelrod's response in *Robert Lowell: Life and Art* is typical:

> Having learned above all else to "write directly about what mattered" to him, Lowell decided to focus on his own dejection and lack of artistic inspiration and to make this very sense of "witheredness" his poetic subject. In place of artistic silence on the one hand, or Ungaretti's lovely "flower gathered" on the other, he produced poems he termed "gathered crumbs." The mood of his book resembles that caught in the title of W. D. Snodgrass's second book: *After Experience*. *For the Union Dead* exposes Lowell's emotional sterility following the conflicts of *Lord Weary's Castle* and the harrowing confessions of *Life Studies*.

William Stafford, writing in *Poetry*, identified in the book "a gift for finding terror and stultification everywhere."

With the exception of the title poem, *For the Union Dead* is an "unpopular" book in the same ways that *Life Studies* is "popular." The title poem, which I will return to shortly, is justly celebrated—a great political ode that masterfully combines the private with the public, the contemporary with the historical, the human with the brute. But one searches the published criticism in vain for competent treatments of many other poems in this volume. A close look at half-a-dozen of them—"The Old Flame," "The Lesson," "Those before Us," "The Drinker," "For the Union Dead," and "The Flaw"—will show that readers have been perhaps too easily put off them because of their difficulty and their inwardness. Yet several of these difficult and often enigmatic poems have more depth and lyricism than the more celebrated *Life Studies* poems, which are painted more broadly, and with a more vivid palette.

Certainly *For the Union Dead* is best read against the background of *Life Studies*, which was published five years earlier. Having explored his madness, rebellion, and private war against society in *Life Studies*, Lowell in *For the Union Dead* may be seen "letting up" a bit, trying to reach some reconciliation with the circumstances of his life, which must often have seemed simply impossible. The violence and rebelliousness are still there, but they are part of Lowell's newfound maturity; his criticism of civilization is even more persuasive than in *Life Studies*, because of its new balance and lack of insistence. Perhaps the most noticeable thing about these poems, against the background of *Life Studies'* forthrightness, is their greater subtlety.

In *Life Studies* Lowell is self-consciously the alienated genius: "I wasn't a child at all— / unseen and all-seeing, I was Agrippina / in the Golden House of Nero . . ." ("My Last Afternoon with Uncle Devereux Winslow"). Yet even in this earlier book he disparages his youthful intensity, including his political activities: "I was a fire-breathing Catholic C.O., / and made my manic statement, / telling off the state and president" ("Memories of West Street and Lepke"). In *For the Union Dead* this chastened, sadly humorous attitude becomes more pronounced.

In "The Old Flame" he disclaims his uniqueness by alluding to the well-known 1940s popular song, "My Old Flame," as a way of writing about his first marriage. The poem opens in a low-key, almost lame tone: "My old flame, my wife! / Remember our lists of birds?" The house he goes back to look at is the one described by Lowell's first wife, Jean Stafford, in "A Country Love Story," in which a young wife and her husband, a middle-aged historian convalescing from tuberculosis, fall out of love. As the wife feels more and more rejected, she gradually gives up plans to remodel the house; to compensate for her loneliness, she invents an imaginary lover.

Ironically, Lowell finds that the house has now *been* restored, but not to suit his taste. The "old flame" is gone, replaced everywhere by new reds that produce a restored-antique kitsch: a 1776 American flag, decorative Indian maize (itself a New England cliché) on the front door, "Atlantic seaboard antique shop / pewter and plunder." The house itself has been freshly painted in "old-red schoolhouse red." One glowing cliché, summed up in John F. Kennedy's slogan, "A new frontier!" The "ghostly / imaginary lover" from Jean Stafford's story is here too, but in the poem he has become suicidal: no one sees him "tighten / the scarf at his throat."

After lampooning the new owners' taste, Lowell goes on to toast them: "Health to the new people, / health to their flag, to their old / restored house on the hill!" And one feels, despite the obvious sarcasm, that there is a large measure of sincerity in these good wishes. Health, because of its elusiveness, is for Lowell a distant beacon. The poem is a somewhat sheepish, only partially ironic celebration, an approving nod in the direction of vulgar normality.

By contrast, Lowell and Stafford are seen as "quivering and fierce," "snowbound together, / simmering like wasps / in our tent of books!"—unhappy, trapped, dangerous. There is a heart-rending sadness in the way the poet invokes his "poor ghost, old love," with her "old voice / of flaming insight / that kept us awake all night." The late-night snowplow, like the "new broom" of the third stanza, parallels the cheerful normality of the new people in contrast to the "snowbound" neurotic writers who hear it "in one bed and apart." Like the renovations on the house, the snowplow can be seen as liberating the couple from their past, "as it tossed off the snow / to the side of the road."

The chastened tone of the verse reinforces the feeling of cold-eyed disenchantment with which Lowell tried, as early as *Life Studies,* to deconstruct the manic, myth-ridden sublimity of his early poetry. The style owes much to the verse of Elizabeth Bishop (who, incidentally, is the woman addressed in the first poem, "Water"). The regular stanzas with their occasional, almost causal rhymes that add little music, give a feeling of subdued sobriety. By contrast, what looks to be free verse in *Life Studies* is a much more musical, with vivid, irregular rhymes and other effects. Both books are, of course, far from the baroque sonority and high rhetoric of *Lord Weary's Castle.* The prevailing tone is one of regret mingled with acceptance.

Compared with a straightforward poem like "The Old Flame," "The Lesson" is almost a riddle. The first tercet invokes a scene from youth:

> No longer to lie reading *Tess of the d'Urbervilles*,
> while the high, mysterious squirrels
> rain small green branches on our sleep!

The present tense "rain" in a scene from the past is only the first peculiarity in this poem. Strange, perhaps, that reading Hardy's *Tess*, one of the bleakest novels ever written, should form part of such a pleasant process. For it is a process, a whole "landscape" of reading and youth that provokes the poet's nostalgia:

> All that landscape, one likes to think it died
> or slept with us, that we ourselves died
> or slept then in the age and second of our habitation.

Unlike the experience of the past in "The Old Flame," evoked with nostalgia but firmly, if half-regretfully, placed in the past, the category "past" here is denied any reality: "The green leaf cushions the same dry footprint . . . and we are where we were." Both present and past are denied separate existence— they are both part of the same moment.

The poem sees the adolescent "landscape" in terms of a lush greenness. The word "died" recurs as the last word of two successive lines, only to be denied. In the lovely phrase, "the age and second of our habitation," Lowell evokes the length and then the brevity of a life—itself made more precise by the latinate "habitation," enforcing a sense that we don't own, we only inhabit. Different forms of the word "sleep" recur with a redundancy that drives the idea into the reader's subconscious awareness, suggesting that the sleeping, or subconscious, mind is where our experience—and "the lesson" derived from it—accumulates. Lowell repeats and emphasizes "We were!" as if, incredulously, to deny it. This poem makes it clear that he is in some ways a mystic, a true heir to the New England Transcendentalists, in his assertion of the eternal present and his denial of time:

> Ah the light lights the window of my young night
> and you never turn off the light,
> while the books lie in the library, and go on reading.

In this poem, the repetition of key words—here "light" re-inforced by the rhyme with "night"—taking on a subsequent anti-rational accretion of meaning, is an important feature.

I once queried Lowell about the "you" in these lines. He replied (in a letter of 12 August 1969): "*You,* I've never quite known; your *one* and quite likely your other interpretations might do, but I felt a tremor of addressing someone loved, a close friend, myself, a girl." Among these choices, it is proba-bly most germane to see "you" as the poet's youthful self, still living—like the squirrels, the landscape, and the books—addressed across the distance of time. Another interesting though marginal reading would make "you" the reader of the poem, who prolongs the poem's and the poet's ghostly life by continuing to introduce it into consciousness.

There is a turn in the last tercet, where pleasant nostalgia gives way to pain:

> The barberry berry sticks on the small hedge,
> cold slits the same crease in the finger,
> the same thorn hurts. The leaf repeats the lesson.

Memory becomes, then, the memory of pain. The Afterword to the first edition of *Notebook* sheds interesting light on the question of whether life for Robert Lowell was an essentially painful experience: "In truth I seem to have felt mostly the joys of living; in remembering, in recording, thanks to the gift of the Muse, it is the pain."

In "Those before Us," which follows "The Lesson" in *For the Union Dead,* Lowell occupies himself with some of the same ideas. Unspecified figures from the past who can reasonably be identified as the aunts, uncles, and grandparents from *Life Studies,* appear:

> They are all outline, uniformly gray,
> unregenerate arrowheads sloughed up by the path here,

or in the corners of the eye, they play
their thankless, fill-in roles. They never were.

Arrowheads—relics from a past civilization—pair up here
with an adjective, "unregenerate," that makes clear just how
far removed these figures are from the continuity of life. The
last phrase of the stanza echoes the previous poem. "They
never were." But this assertion is vain, as the next stanza
shows, because their ghostly figures continue to occupy the
summer cottage where the poem is set—a summer-cottage
atmosphere familiar to readers of *Life Studies,* where, in "My
Last Afternoon with Uncle Devereux Winslow," Lowell so viv-
idly evoked his grandfather's "farm," or summer place, seen
through a child's wondering eyes:

> What were those sunflowers? Pumpkins floating shoulder-
>   high?
> It was sunset, Sadie and Nellie
> bearing pitchers of ice-tea,
> oranges, lemons, mint, and peppermints,
> and the jug of shandygaff,
> which Grandpa made by blending half and half
> yeasty, wheezing homemade sarsaparilla with beer.

The idyll in that poem is violated by the sense of lurking death:

> No one had died there in my lifetime . . .
> Only Cinder, our Scottie puppy
> paralysed from gobbling toads.

In "Those before Us" a fierce and bizarre kind of violence
erupts within an otherwise comfortable domestic situation:
"The muskrat that took a slice of your thumb still huddles, /
a mop of hair and a heart-beat on the porch." This violence
tucked away within the family is present in practically every-
thing Lowell wrote. Thomas Parkinson discusses, in *Robert
Lowell: A Collection of Critical Essays,* "the crucial metaphor of
the animal":

> Domesticated animals are monsters. Beasts associated with
> men become more or less than beasts—dogs, rats, chickens,

pigs are all revolting as ideas, however charming any single specimen may be. They are parodies and realizations of our natures. *For the Union Dead* is full of animals that have been made monstrous by human tones and cagings. The muskrat that slices the poet's thumb and smashes a wooden crate to pieces in its furious frustration is not an animal but a being made monstrous by human impositions.

The poem goes directly, without transition, from the muskrat to the ancestral figures:

> Their chairs were *ex cathedra*, yet if you draw back the blinds,
> (as full of windows as a fishnet now)
> you will hear them conspiring, slapping hands
> across the bent card-table, still leaf-green.

Are these ancestors, or the card-table, "leaf-green"? The ambiguity is characteristic. That they are dead (though still present) makes them less formidable, and Lowell expresses the unmixed urge to be reconciled with their memory, in contrast to "Grandparents" from *Life Studies*, where feelings of guilt and rebellion still cloud his recollections:

> Grandpa! Have me, hold me, cherish me!
> Tears smut my fingers. There
> half my life-lease later,
> I hold an *Illustrated London News*—
> disloyal still,
> I doodle handlebar
> mustaches on the last Russian Czar.

Unlike the grandparents in *Life Studies*, formidable enough to be associated with the Czar of Russia, commanding enough as parental authorities to be "disloyal" to, the ghosts here are simply human, vulnerable: "some one lets out his belt to breathe, some one / roams in negligee. Bless the confidence / of their sitting unguarded there in stocking feet." One hardly doubts the existence of these ghosts; in a pun that might be drawn from the title, they are squarely "before us." Time stands still in this poem. Then, as happens after one experiences a moment outside time, time starts up again:

> Sands drop from the hour-glass waist and swallow tail.
> We follow their gunshy shadows down the trail—
> those before us! Pardon them for existing.
> We have stopped watching them. They have stopped
>   watching.

In a delicate image of Edwardian ladies and gentlemen, where "Sands drop from the hourglass waist and swallow tail," the passage of time becomes brilliantly visual. The timeless moment is over: one breathes again. Lowell sees the ancestors now as figures who precede us into the future—we are behind them in this journey: "those before us!" Another twist on the word *before*. It is not true that "They never were." Lowell excels in the subtlety with which he handles grammar. "Pardon them for existing" in the next-to-last line is and is not the same as "Pardon them for having existed." The poem invokes the ancestors for the purpose of exorcising them, and this would not be necessary if "They never were," as the first stanza claims. But the same mood of forgiveness and tender compassion that is present in "The Old Flame" prevails here.

Lowell again concerns himself with time in "The Drinker," where the abrupt first line jolts us: "The man is killing time— there's nothing else." In *Life Studies,* material of this nature was treated as personal revelation and presented in the first person. I say "treated" because the *Life Studies* poems give a deceptive impression of being more faithfully autobiographical—as they were taken to be at the time—than they actually turn out to have been. Lowell made this point as early as 1961 in a *Paris Review* interview, "The Art of Poetry: Robert Lowell," with Frederick Seidel: "They're not always factually true. There's a good deal of tinkering with fact. You leave out a lot, and emphasize this and not that. Your actual experience is a complete flux. I've invented facts and changed things, and the whole balance of the poem was something invented."

The shocking detail from the *Life Studies* poem "To Speak

of Woe That Is in Marriage"—"Each night now I tie / ten dollars and his car key to my thigh" (the wife in the poem is speaking)—is borrowed, one learns, from the wife of Delmore Schwartz, Lowell's contemporary. In context, however, and following "Man and Wife," which is clearly about Lowell's own marriage to Elizabeth Hardwick, any reader would approach the poem according to the ground rules of Confessional poetry, which was heralded as liberating American poetry from artifice and the use of the persona. All of this, we were led to understand by critics like M. L. Rosenthal, who coined the term Confessional poetry, was the raw, unvarnished truth. The experience is further contextualized by the last two lines of the poem: "Gored by the climacteric of his want, / he stalls above me like an elephant." The prose piece, "91 Revere Street," uses the same unusual word in an unlikely context that makes it stand out:

> Once Commander Billy sprawled back so recklessly that the armchair began to come apart. "You see, Charlotte," he said to Mother, "at the height of my *climacteric* I am breaking Bob's chair."

Regarded as a type, "the drinker" of this poem is a pathetic victim, imagined in terms reminiscent of the whales in "The Quaker Graveyard":

> No help from his body, the whale's
> warm-hearted blubber, foundering down
> leagues of ocean, gasping whiteness.
> The barbed hooks fester. The lines snap tight.

Chief among his troubles, though, is his isolation. When he thinks of turning to his neighbors, "their names blur in the window." As always, Lowell's images and ideas are never less than precise: When he writes that "His despair has the galvanized color / of the mop and water in the galvanized bucket," it may be of interest to recall that to galvanize metal is to treat it with rust-resistant zinc so that no chemical reaction is possible between water and metal. This qualifies and rescues from bathos the lines about his wife: "Once she was close to him / as water to the dead metal," which sound like the ruminations of a self-pitying drunk.

The proposition here, though, is whether one can kill time. As the poem progresses, instances of the passage of time are introduced—innocently, almost. There are "her engagements inked on her calendar," which the drinker regards as "a list of indictments." Despite his relentless solipsism, despite the good offices of "the fifth of Bourbon / chucked helter-skelter into the river," time passes: "The cheese wilts in the rat-trap / the milk turns to junket in the cornflakes bowl." Two ways out, escape and suicide, suggest themselves: "car keys and razor blades / shine in an ashtray." And at this point the poem's opening proposition is raised again, this time in the form of a question:

> Is he killing time? Out on the street,
> two cops on horseback clop through the April rain
> to check the parking meter violations—
> their oilskins yellow as forsythia.

Reality, of a sort, interposes itself between the drinker and his problems—a denouement that is perhaps inevitable in the solipsist's world. This ending is very like the ending of "Skunk Hour," where the family of skunks appears and resolves the poet's obsession with his own self-destructive fantasies. The mounted policemen, with the wholesome "clop" of their horses' hooves in the freshness of the April rain, seem to say to the drinker: Get moving; the time you have paid for is used up. With the beautiful simile of their forsythia-colored slickers, they too are an image of time passing—they are the unlikely harbingers of spring.

The book's title poem, the much-anthologized "For the Union Dead," presents itself as a public poem and was in fact commissioned to be read at the Boston Arts Festival in 1960. Originally called "Colonel Shaw and the Massachusetts 54th," what will turn out to be a celebration of the young officer and his black Civil War regiment starts at a slant, with a lament for the South Boston Aquarium, closed now, which "stands / in a

Sahara of snow." Lowell's nostalgia for the predatory, subhuman world that held great appeal for him—"I often sigh still / for the dark downward and vegetating kingdom / of the fish and reptile"—finds an object in the Boston Common, where excavations are being carried out:

> Behind their cage,
> yellow dinosaur steamshovels were grunting
> as they cropped up tons of mush and grass
> to gouge their underworld garage.

The sequence in which successive elements of the poem are presented suggests that while the aquarium has been closed, the "dark downward and vegetating kingdom" has spilled out onto the Boston Common, traditionally the city's symbolic and actual civic center. The garage is "underworld," not just underground: according to newspapers at the time, the Mafia had its hands deep in the city's pockets. In a poem about civic virtue, what are being created here are parking spaces "like civic / sandpiles." The city's ancient probity has been trivialized. The poem entertains, through description, the past as parody: "A girdle of orange, Puritan-pumpkin colored girders / braces the tingling Statehouse."

Readers of Lowell's very early poetry will recall his role as a Jeremiah, a riddling prophet of the Apocalypse sent to restore his city to the ancient virtues it has lost:

> I saw the sky descending, black and white,
> Not blue, on Boston where the winters wore
> The skulls to jack-o'-lanterns on the slates,
> . . . .
> And I am a red arrow on this graph
> Of Revelations. Every dove is sold
> The Chapel's sharp-shinned eagle shifts its hold
> On serpent-Time, the rainbow's epitaph.
>
> > "Where the Rainbow Ends"

The jack-o'-lanterns of the earlier poetry return as a parody in "Puritan-pumpkin" color, a child's crayon drawing of the New England past.

Literally peripheral to the corrupt gouging of the present, St. Gaudens's bronze Civil War relief of the Colonel and his troops, set aside while the work proceeds, is "shaking," "propped by a plank splint against the garage's earthquake." Yet it upbraids the present and "sticks like a fishbone / in the city's throat." Shaw is "as lean / as a compass-needle," pointing the city in a direction it has lost. If, as Thomas Parkinson asserts, "*For the Union Dead* is full of animals that have been made monstrous by human tones and cagings," Colonel Shaw is presented with healthy animal qualities: "He has an angry wrenlike vigilance, / a greyhound's gentle tautness." With an old-fashioned aristocratic austerity, "he seems to wince at pleasure, / and suffocate for privacy." Clearly the writer here is the same man who, in a letter to his mother exactly twenty years earlier, had defended his values as "taking the intellect and aristocracy and family tradition seriously." But the constraints self-imposed on the aristocratic personality are not ignored: "when he leads his black soldiers to death, / he cannot bend his back."

If Lowell in his madness was drawn to tyrants, when he was himself he came down solidly behind all that is good about the American political tradition, and especially *noblesse oblige*, the obligation of the fortunate and gifted to serve the people, as Bobby Kennedy was willing to do: "For them like a prince, you daily left your tower / to walk through dirt in your best cloth."

While Colonel Shaw "rejoices in man's lovely, / peculiar power to choose life and die," Lowell sees the national mood at the height of the Cold War as a determination to choose death in the form of nuclear brinkmanship and live with it, as hinted at by the advertisement which "shows Hiroshima boiling // over a Mosler Safe, the 'Rock of Ages' / that survived the blast." Colonel Shaw, "riding on his bubble" of aristocratic values that constrain him at the same time they enable him, "waits," somewhat mysteriously, "for the blessèd break"—the appealing relief that for Lowell on some deep level is associated with the end of the world. He is still in some measure the prophet of Apocalypse who would like to bring the world down around him, as well as being "the little muddler" of his "Child's Song," who "can't stand itself."

The reader who knows Lowell primarily through his political poems may be surprised by "The Lesson" and "Those before Us," which entertain mystical notions and suggest a transcendental stance toward time. His ambiguous (in the Empsonian sense) use of language stretches one's narrow (or if you prefer, realistic) ideas about the limits of time and of life and death. Lowell's essentially religious nature did not become completely secular upon his apostasy from Catholicism in the late 1940s. He once claimed that *Life Studies* was a more religious book than the openly Catholic *Lord Weary's Castle:* I think he meant that there was more compassion in it. I have already mentioned Lowell's affinity with the New England Transcendentalists. "The Flaw" deals directly with theological questions and is at the same time a love poem.

The poem begins with a favorite symbol of Lowell's: a seal. In harmony with the conditions of its life, not conscious of itself as something that will die, it manages a heavy surf in fun, like a swimming poodle. With an abrupt transition, the scene changes from this icy-cold, invigorating picture to a country graveyard in a heat wave: life and death in dramatic contrast. In an interesting reversal, heat is associated here with death, cold with life. The graveyard is like a heat mirage where "Some mote, some eye-flaw, wobbles in the heat, / hair-thin, hair-dark, the fragment of a hair— // a noose, a question?" Is it in the air or in the eye? The poem makes complex theological allusions against the background, laid down in the first stanza, of the seal and the country graveyard. According to Bishop Berkeley and the Puritan theologian Jonathan Edwards, the world and man's soul exist in the eye of God. God sees man, but man is free to choose his own course of action: "if there's free will, it's something like this hair, / inside my eye, outside my eye, yet free, / airless as grace if the good God . . . I see."

If we filled the ellipsis in, Lowell would seem to be asking: What if God shut his eye? Then we and the world would cease to exist. To put the argument another way, the world exists as a thought in the mind of God; and if God's mind should wander? "Our bodies quiver." In fear or in excitement? "In this rustling air, / all's possible, all's unpredictable." The thing that makes what Lowell is doing impressive is his ability to include so many elements in the mix. Here, in a vividly rendered setting, he carries on a compelling meditation on complex questions—relating them, as they must finally be related, to the lives of people. "Old wives and husbands! Look, their gravestones wait / in couples with the names and half the date— / one future and one freedom." Is the "one future" death? Is the "one freedom" the freedom to die? Or is there more? Lowell argues neither atheism nor belief, but takes the position that we don't really know. In a deathly parody of the happy, oblivious seal, the couple's "eager, sharpened cries" become surrealistically "a pair of stones, / cutting like shark-fins though the boundless wash."

Lowell makes himself and his wife, like the shadow figures in "Those before Us," pathetic and ghostlike in their insubstantiality. These shadows have human passions, act like humans, but you can see right through them: "Two walking cobwebs, almost bodiless, / crossed paths here once, kept house, and lay in beds." The language is really too rich to yield easily to explication, but the poem has the effect of reducing human life to the essential: "our bodies, grown insensible, / ready to dwindle off into the soul, / two motes or eye-flaws." The biblical associations of the word "mote" are crucial, lending an air of pessimism about human life, since in Matthew 7:3–4, the "mote" is something to be cast out of the eye:

And why beholdest thou the mote that is in thy brother's eye, but considerest not the beam that is in thine own eye?
Or how wilt thou say to thy brother, Let me pull out the mote out of thine eye; and, behold, a beam is in thine own eye?

The human soul here becomes the mote, or flaw, in God's eye—all part of Lowell's insistence that human life is in essence tragically flawed. So what little hope we have is in "the invisible . . . Hope of the hopeless."

One's sense of the meaning of the title keeps changing throughout the poem: man is himself the flaw; yet of course death is "the great flaw" in our lives. On the other hand, death "gives the final gift." Does that gift simply release us from a life of pain, or is it the gift of immortality? Lowell poses these questions elusively and yet compellingly—always within a human context. The closing couplet, playing on the conceit of the eye-flaw ("a noose, a question?") concludes the poem, inevitably, on a note of doubt. But it is a quintessentially human doubt, informed by pathos and tenderness: "Dear Figure curving like a questionmark, / how will you hear my answer in the dark?"

Lowell's gloom is not facile: it arises from deep reflection. Yet as these six poems make clear, there is considerable hope, humor, and compassion in his poetry. His complexity is not a surface feature, but rather an outgrowth of his thought, which is supple and searching. If his poems are often enigmatic, they mirror his conclusions about the enigmatic nature of existence.

Obsessions of the
"Tragic Generation"

I'm cross with god who has wrecked this generation.
First he siezed Ted, then Richard, Randall, and now Delmore.
In between he gorged on Sylvia Plath.
That was a first rate haul. He left alive
fools I could number like a kitchen knife
but Lowell he did not touch.

—John Berryman, "Dream Song #153"

Were they killed, as standard radicals say, by our corrupted
society?

—Robert Lowell, "For John Berryman, 1914–1972"

I used to want to live
to avoid your elegy.
Yet really we had the same life,
the generic one
our generation offered
(Les Maudits—the compliment
each American generation
pays itself in passing)
. . . .
We asked to be obsessed with writing,
and we were.

—Robert Lowell, "For John Berryman"

Three American poets who, like Lowell, were born around the
time of World War I and died in the sixties and seventies—
John Berryman, Delmore Schwartz, and Randall Jarrell—
have, through a series of recent biographies, ironically become
known to a wider audience than ever read their poetry. These
biographies include *Delmore Schwartz: The Life of an American*

Poet, by James Atlas; *Robert Lowell,* by Ian Hamilton, which I examined in an earlier essay; as well as *Dream Song: The Life of John Berryman* by Paul Mariani, who has recently also published his own biography of Lowell; and *The Life of John Berryman* by John Haffenden. Perhaps most tellingly, though—because both the idea suggested in its title and the approach taken in the book itself represent an attempt to make a statement about their generic lives—a picture of these men emerges from *Poets in Their Youth* by Eileen Simpson, Berryman's first wife, that justifies their characterization, as Yeats said of the English poets of the 1890s, as "the tragic generation." The spectacle of their lives may inspire a reaction—particularly in other writers—to use Aristotle's formulation about tragedy, "pity and terror."

Much that can be said about these four men can also be said of R. P. Blackmur, who, although not remarkable as a poet, was an important critic and mentor for Berryman and Schwartz. Theodore (Ted) Roethke, a few years older and most of the time geographically removed from his contemporaries on the East coast, was another brilliant poet plagued by alcoholism and mental illness. Dylan Thomas was also of this generation and, though a Welshman, met his downfall in America. Berryman saw a lot of him in England as a student at Clare College, Cambridge, and his sense that any poet worth his salt had to be a hard drinker must have been a formative influence on Berryman's own drinking. If we consider these men as victims of American attitudes toward poetry, then Thomas must be included. Though the whisky that caused "acute insult to the brain" and killed him at thirty-nine was distilled in the British Isles, the money that paid for it, the encouragement of Dylan Thomas in his role as self-destructive *poète maudit,* was made in America. Among slightly younger poets one must include Sylvia Plath and Anne Sexton.

Why was life a tragedy for these greatly gifted poets? Did they really lead "the same life," as Lowell wrote about Berryman, "the generic one / our generation offered?" And is *"maudit"*—"damned"—the best way to describe them? A popular theory makes them victims of American philistinism. Berryman and Schwartz were talking along these lines fifty years ago. (I quote here and elsewhere from *Poets in Their Youth,* unless otherwise indicated): "Delmore and he had been born at the wrong time and in the wrong country. 'Pushkin could count on railway workers to know his poems. Think of it! Who reads poetry in America?' " The American Left's infatuation with things Russian informs Schwartz's citation of Pushkin. In the last days of the Soviet Union one began to get a bit tired of hearing how a poetry reading by Yevtushenko could fill a Soviet football stadium. The neglect argument is familiar to contemporary poets—and finally rejected by most that I know of. Rather than suffering from neglect, Dylan Thomas, after all, suffered from a surfeit of attention—attention of the wrong, celebrity sort. Certainly Schwartz and Jarrell, and Berryman early in his career, were wounded by neglect—Lowell much less so, since he became the most honored serious poet of his day.

In a turn that few would have predicted early on, Lowell became the survivor of the group. The deaths of his friends hit him hard. When Berryman died in 1972, Lowell, having outlived them all, was moved to write: "Jarrell's death was the sadder. If it hadn't happened, it wouldn't have happened. He would be with me now, in full power, as far as one may at fifty. This might-have-been (it's a frequent thought) stings my eyes. John, with pain and joy like his friend Dylan Thomas, almost won what he gambled for." The lives and deaths of his fellow "poets of personal extremity," a more sophisticated and accurate formulation than "Confessional poets," had clearly been on his mind, particularly from his position of self-imposed exile in England. These remarks, included in his elegy for Berryman in the *New York Review of Books,* are pointed and uncharacteristically caustic:

> I must say something of death and the *extremist poets,* as we are named in often pre-funerary tributes. Except for Weldon Kees and Sylvia Plath, they lived as long as Shakespeare, outlived Wyatt, Baudelaire, and Hopkins, and long outlived the forever Romantics, those who really died young. John himself lived to the age of Beethoven, whom he celebrates in the most ambitious and perhaps finest of his late poems, a monument to his long love, unhampered expression, and subtle criticism.

John died with fewer infirmities than Beethoven. The consolation somehow doesn't wash. I feel the jagged gash with which my contemporaries died, with which we were to die. Were they killed, as standard radicals say, by our corrupted society? Was their success an aspect of their destruction? Were we uncomfortable epigoni of Frost, Pount, Eliot, Marianne Moore, etc.? This bitter possibility came to us at the moment of our *arrival*. Death comes sooner or later, these made it sooner.

To look at the practical details: Academic employment, which turns many writers into rootless nomads detached from their native communities, had as some of its first beneficiaries and victims Berryman, Lowell, and company: "The game of poetical chairs—in which writers moved from campus to campus, pausing for shorter or longer periods depending on the whim of the whistle-blower, then moving on to another chair—came in to fashion in the early fifties." The uncertainty of this existence, as well as what may strike us now as quixotic resentment against American culture—or the lack of it, if one is using the word to mean an appreciation of high art—surely rubbed salt into Berryman's already serious (in retrospect, fatal) psychic wounds: "What kind of man was it who, with his intelligence and education . . . couldn't support a wife? The fault must be his. He was in some way responsible. The burden of guilt, never light, that he carried around, had become so crushing that he could hardly drag himself out of bed in the morning." One is hard put not to agree with Berryman's sister-in-law, speaking in 1952: "There's nothing so much the matter with John that a little recognition wouldn't cure." Another familiar circumstance—that one can get decent pay for teaching, writing book reviews and travel articles, etc., giving poetry readings, but not, except when the occasional grant comes along, for writing poetry—is evident in Simpson's book, as we see Berryman leaping dangerously from one temporary job, fellowship, or writing assignment to the next.

Many contemporary writers worry over the uncertainty of their livelihoods. I have seen friends agonize, become bitter and even unhinged, wondering where money for rent and groceries would come from. But writers of our own time, having been brought up on the literary-political status quo, have had more time to adjust to it than Berryman's generation—the generation, that is, who began to publish and teach during the 1940s and 1950s. Berryman, Schwartz, Lowell, Jarrell, et al., were the first to experience the still-prevailing *modus operandi* of the academic and publishing worlds, and because they brought more idealistic standards to the scene, were the more crashingly disillusioned. Besides, the creative writing industry has flourished, to the extent that some writing programs even pay the bills for their former patrons, the professors of literature. A writer's life in America is by no means serene, but on the whole one knows what to expect, even if one expects little. That is why I call today's writers (not excluding myself) the "laid-back" generation.

Still, appealing as it may be, blaming the cultural vacuity of the United States for these men's unhappy lives is, as Lowell says of the views of "standard radicals," a little too easy. Berryman, for example, had achieved recognition and financial security by the time he killed himself. Lowell and Schwartz would probably have been mad no matter what, and to call Berryman and Jarrell "unstable" by nature is a pathetic understatement. We do not know how their lives would have turned out in what Jarrell called "that Yesterday in which people stood on chairs to look at Lord Tennyson." The family's role in the etiology of emotional disturbance has not been firmly established, but it would have been hard, even for writers as inventive as these four, to have dreamed up more damaging parents than we know Lowell, Berryman, and Schwartz to have had.

Lowell's mother, whom his first wife, Jean Stafford, referred to as "Charlotte Hideous," managed to tyrannize her son and sheepish husband thoroughly. Her son's heroic struggle to become independent was a damaging ordeal. Lowell shared with Berryman and Schwartz the experience of being kept awake at night by his parents' quarrels. Schwartz's father was an expansive, philandering real-estate entrepreneur who abandoned his wife and family early on. (Little has been written on Jarrell's parents except that they were divorced when he was very young.) If we want to find a common ground for these four poets, the family, not the society, would seem to be the place to look.

"One day, Daddy," Berryman told Eileen Simpson, "agitated and depressed [after the failure of his Florida real-estate schemes] took me on his back and swam far out in the Gulf at Clearwater, threatening to drown us both. *Or so Mother claimed* [my italics] . . . Early one morning he got out his gun and put a bullet through his head." The suicide of John Allyn Smith (Berryman was the name of his mother's second husband, who adopted John and his brother), which occurred when Berryman was twelve, haunted him for the rest of his life. Ultimately, he leapt off a bridge into the frozen Mississippi on January 7, 1972, at the age of fifty-seven. Eileen Simpson saw this suicide prefigured early on:

> Before our marriage, I had worried about our relationship being threatened by his "unspeakably powerful possessive adoring MOTHER." After the night on the esplanade [when Berryman first hinted at suicide] I became aware of the presence of a tall mute shadowy figure whose features I could not make out, a figure whose power over John was as strong as his mother's. It was the power of John Allyn Smith.

Lowell's life was, a lot of the time, nightmarish. After recurrent mental breakdowns, domestic lacerations, shock treatment, and years of medication for bipolar disorder he died of a heart attack—prematurely, really—at sixty. Jarrell threw himself in front of a car on a North Carolina highway at fifty-one. Schwartz, fifty-three, died of a heart attack, alone, agonizingly, in a Times Square fleabag hotel, his body going unclaimed in the morgue for three days because, as Saul Bellow wrote, "there were no readers of modern poetry" around to make the identification. These ghastly historics arc familiar to many readers—more familiar, again, than the poetry these men wrote.

Was being poets what killed them? The evidence, on the contrary, is that poetry saved them—to the extent that they could be, and were, saved. This is apparently what Eileen Simpson thought about Berryman:

> It was the poetry that had kept him alive. His father had committed suicide at forty. With as much reason, and with a similar psychic makeup, John had been tempted more than once to follow his father's example. That he lived seventeen years longer than [his father], that he died a "veteran of life," was thanks to his gift. It had not been the hand coaxing him down from the railing that had brought him back each time, he now believed, but the certainty that there were all those poems to be written.

Jarrell, though perhaps not of the first rank as a poet, was the greatest practical critic and wickedest literary wit of his time. Lowell and Berryman approached greatness. Of the four, Delmore Schwartz is the only utter tragedy, for the gin, the paranoia, and the amphetamines that destroyed him as a person also destroyed him as an artist. He had been famous before his three friends had even broken into print. Allen Tate called his poetry "the first real innovation we've had since Eliot and Pound."

Lowell's poem, "To Delmore Schwartz," with an epigraph placing the events in "Cambridge 1946," begins on a note disparaging the poets' lack of grasp on practical realities—"We couldn't even keep the furnace lit!"—and goes on to refer to "our long maneuvered visit / from T. S. Eliot's brother, Henry Ware." (Delmore Schwartz prided himself on being a great literary politician. Berryman's nickname for him was Machiavelli.) With his gift for using inanimate objects to adumbrate personality—its clearest expression can be found in the way he makes family furniture come alive in "91 Revere Street"—Lowell catches the reader by surprise with the abrupt introduction of Delmore's mounted duck:

> Your stuffed duck craned toward Harvard from my trunk:
> its bill was a black whistle, and its brow
> was high and thinner than a baby's thumb;
> its webs were tough as toenails on its bough.
> It was your first kill; you had rushed it home,
> pickled in a tin wastebasket of rum—
> it looked through us, as if it'd died dead drunk.

The duck represents the young men's ambivalence toward the authority of Harvard: a kind of yearning and a weird defiance. It also seems the perfect emblem of the two poets: "it lived with us and met our stare, / Rabelaisian, lubricious, drugged." The three adjectives dangling at the end of the clause are positioned to modify either the duck or the poets, or both.

Schwartz was a great fabulist who entertained his friends with outrageous fantasies about T. S. Eliot's sex life, and about the *Partisan Review* crowd and all of literary New York. The notion of pickling a dead duck in a "tin wastebasket of rum" is not much more unlikely than his translation of Rimbaud's *Une Saison en Enfer,* in which he rendered "*Je revais, je revais*" as "I review, I review." Lowell's poem revels in the same degree of wild exaggeration in his depiction of Schwartz's Cambridge digs, where the "antiquated / refrigerator gurgled mustard gas / through your mustard-yellow house." The tone partakes of the same self-satire that makes the reader a bit uneasy in a poem like "Memories of West Street and Lepke." Here, the dead duck "cooled our universal / *Angst* a moment."

Perhaps only Schwartz, playing on the meaning of the German word *freud* and the partial rhyme between their names, would associate Joyce and Freud with joy: "Let Joyce and Freud, / the Masters of Joy, / be our guests here" is the toast he proposes. Having paralleled the two young writers with the word-intoxicated modernist and the founder of psychoanalysis, Lowell brings in a more dangerous master:

> The room was filled
> with cigarette smoke circling the paranoid,
> inert gaze of Coleridge, back
> from Malta—his eyes lost in flesh, lips baked and black.

Coleridge represents a tragically apt parallel for Schwartz, since he too faced a future of paranoia and drug addiction.

Like Coleridge's life, like Schwartz's life, Lowell's poem is a study in disintegration. The first two lines are a largely regular iambic pentameter couplet with full rhymes: "We couldn't even keep the furnace lit! / Even when we had disconnected it." A scansion of the poem reveals an iambic rhythm that gets more and more irregular as the poem goes along. The rhyming couplets lapse into some very hit-or-miss effects, ending with:

> In the ebb-
> light of morning, we stuck
> the duck
> -'s web-
> foot, like a candle, in a quart of gin we'd killed.

The overall effect imitates an all-night session of gin and talk between these *poètes maudits,* during the course of which Delmore quotes the lines from Wordsworth that were a kind of motto for him and John Berryman: changing, in the first line, "gladness" to "sadness," and then in the second line, "sadness" to "madness":

> You said:
> *"We poets in our youth begin in sadness;*
> *thereof in the end come despondency and madness;*
> Stalin has had two cerebral hemorrhages!"

The reader, particularly the reader forty years after the events described in the poem, must wonder what the logic of all this is—though to look for logic in this poem would be to look for something that is not intended. Are Stalin's cerebral hemorrhages (he would not die until 1953) cause for celebration or sorrow? As the *Partisan Review* era, and the American literary scene's love affair with left-wing politics and idealization of Soviet Communism, recedes further into the past, it is hard to answer the question with certainty. The poem, with Schwartz's ironic toast, its drunken atmosphere of paranoia and alienation, leads nowhere—and that is its very point.

Berryman's poetry was, to a very large extent, elegiac. If one compares one of the ten Dream Songs he wrote about Delmore Schwartz to Lowell's poem, what emerges is a much more pointed attitude:

This world is gradually becoming a place
where I do not care to be any more. Can Delmore die?
I don't suppose
in all them years a day went ever by
without a loving thought for him. Welladay.
In the brightness of his promise,

unstained, I saw him thro' the mist of the actual
blazing with insight, warm with gossip
thro' all our Harvard years
when both of us were just becoming known.
I got him out of a police-station once, in Washington, the
    world is *tref*
and grief too astray for tears.

I imagine you have heard the terrible news,
that Delmore Schwartz is dead, miserably & alone,
in New York: he sang me a song
'I am the Brooklyn poet Delmore Schwartz
Harms & the child I sing, two parents' torts'
when he was young & gift-strong.

Viewed along the curve of Berryman's death wish, his friend's death strengthens his own inclination toward suicide. Remembering the way he characterizes his alter ego as "Huffy Henry," one could say that Berryman in the first two lines adopts a rather huffy attitude toward the world itself: "a place / where I do not care to be any more." "The actual" is, in his words, only "a mist" anyway. By quoting Delmore's own parody of the first line of the *Aeneid* about "Harms & the child," following it up with the bizarre rhyme Schwartz/torts, this Dream Song lays the blame for Delmore's tragic life at the feet of the family—unlike the stanza from Berryman I quoted at the beginning of this chapter, which blames "god."

By saying that "the world is *tref*" (unkosher, ritually impure), Berryman, who regarded himself as, to quote the title of one of his short stories, "An Imaginary Jew," feels free to assume Schwartz's Jewish identity as his own: an example of what Lowell called his "impertinent piety." In the *Dream Songs*, he felt equally free to write, as it were, in blackface. These gestures seem to be as presumptuous as Sylvia Plath's assumed Jewishness in "Daddy":

> An engine, an engine
> Chuffing me off like a Jew.
> A Jew to Dachau, Auschwitz, Belsen.
> I began to talk like a Jew.
> I think I may well be a Jew.

Some would evoke art's right to be presumptuous. Whatever the merits of that argument, here it is more pertinent to make the point that Berryman's gesture is one more way of holding the world at arm's length. One more step in the process of alienation that gets between Berryman's poems and many readers.

> *We asked to be obsessed with writing,*
> *and we were.*
>
> *Couldn't Lowell understand that others simply didn't live for*
> *poetry the way he did?*

The second of these quotations, from an *Atlantic Monthly* piece about studying with Robert Lowell at Harvard, is what James Atlas thought after a long liquid lunch with his teacher at the Iruña in Cambridge. It was precisely, however, Lowell's ability to inspire a sense of artistic perfectionism, of the necessity to live and breathe poetry, that was his priceless gift to younger writers. The word *obsession* crops up often, too, in *Poets in Their Youth*, Eileen Simpson's account of Berryman and his friends. I'm afraid I cannot agree with the writers of blurbs and reviewers at the time it appeared who called this book "exquisitely tender," "kind," "sympathetic." It has that surface. But beneath Eileen Simpson's affectionate tone, she condescends, presenting the poets as difficult but charming eccentrics:

Having anthologies by heart, John and Cal had no need for books. . . .
"What are [Yeats's] three greatest lines?"
"Greatest lines? Must we select?" John fought this narrowness.
"Cal gets that from Randall," Jean said, not quite sotto voce

and looking as if she'd swallowed her tongue. "Randall has a passion for The Three Greatest. Cal's caught it."

Cal, scowling with concentration . . . wouldn't be deflected: They must find the three greatest lines.

John said, "I'll give you six instead:

> Unwearied still, lover by lover,
> They paddle in the cold
> Companionable streams or climb the air;
> Their hearts have not grown old;
> Passion or conquest, wander where they will,
> Attend upon them still."

. . . We must stay, Cal said. How could John even consider going when they hadn't discussed "Lycidas"?

Everyone who knew Lowell at all well got a taste of his "three greatest lines" routine. To people who are not particularly interested in poetry, it would no doubt have seemed peculiar and probably boring. But if you were trying to educate your taste, then it was a valuable exercise. One summer I was driving him up to his summer place in Castine, Maine. He pointed to an overpass we were approaching and asked, "How would you describe that?" When I couldn't come up with anything, he began ad-libbing descriptions of the overpass. His famous three-adjective combinations were an exercise he found endlessly fascinating. "Diamond-pointed, athirst and Norman," "neurasthenic, scarlet and wild," and "Rabelaisian, lubricious, drugged," which I quoted above, are three from *Life Studies*. On that same trip to Maine I came up with "green, inarticulate, subterranean," which I later used in a poem, and "wigged-out, buck-naked, and barely audible," for which I have yet to find a suitable context.

During one of the rain delays in last year's baseball playoffs, the local TV station showed a thirty-minute film on batting, featuring Ted Williams. It was an eye-opener for me: I usually just get up there and swing. Ted Williams talked in minute detail about the virtues of different stances: when one stance was appropriate and when not; how young hitters should practice swinging—without the ball—at different parts of the

strike zone. He said he was surprised that young players sel-
dom tried to guess what the next pitch would be, he spoke at
length on the rotation of the hips, etc., etc. This man was
obsessed! His lifetime batting average was .344, with 521
home runs. In 1941 he batted .406.

Have we in the "laid-back" generation lost something? This
is not the rhetorical question it may seem. By comparison with
the poets of the 1950s, it may be said in our favor that we have
"joined the human race" and shed the anti-American, pseudo-
European snobbery that was almost a reflex for intellectuals
and writers of Berryman's era: " 'How much easier it would be
if we were abroad,' he'd say. 'Now if we were in Paris, we could
go to La Coupole,' Or, 'If we were in London . . . ' "

Perhaps coming to terms with America gives our writing the
vital possibility of becoming a national literature, something
that could not be said of most of the poetry of the 1950s, when
our writers' imaginations, like their taste buds and their sum-
mers, belonged to Europe. But our laudable efforts to bring
poetry closer to "the people" ("Poetry is not a matter of a few,"
advertisements for the *American Poetry Review* say) often end up
giving "the people" something less than poetry. In *APR,* for
instance, the photographs of attractive young women wearing
partially unbuttoned blouses and burly, bearded men in work
shirts are often more arresting than the poetry these photo-
genic persons write. Can it be that we are so used to hearing
about the public's disregard for poetry that we have started to
internalize this disregard and even to become apologetic about
our vocation? If poets do not believe that poetry has, at least
potentially, something of vital importance to offer society, then
that something will disappear.

What a distance we are from the high claims made by Ran-
dall Jarrell forty years ago in "The Obscurity of the Poet"
from *Poetry and the Age:*

> Art matters not merely because it is the most magnificent orna-
> ment and the most nearly unfailing occupation of our lives, but
> because it is life itself. From Christ to Freud we have believed
> that, if we know the truth, the truth will set us free: art is
> indispensable because so much of this truth can be learned

through works of art and through works of art alone—for which of us could have learned for himself what Proust and Chekhov, Hardy and Yeats and Rilke, Shakespeare and Homer learned for us?

... Human life without some form of poetry is not human life but animal existence.

That art teaches us about life is an idea seldom heard from poets now, and never from the exponents of "critical theory." From reading texts, they say, we only learn about other texts.

The task, it seems to me, is to avoid the temptation toward despair and self-destructiveness that so damaged the lives of the "tragic" generation, while at the same time taking seriously their dedication to the redemptive value of poetry. Lowell, in an elegiac tribute to Jarrell, used the word "noble" to describe his old friend. John Berryman had his own fierce nobility, which he characteristically hid under self-satire.

His single-minded obsession with poetry, his gift for transforming his own brilliance and his own pain into art—these enabled him to leave behind a tortured but strangely sublime and moving testament.

> Henry's pelt was put on sundry walls
> where it did much resemble Henry and
> them persons was delighted.
> Especially his long & glowing tail
> by all them was admired, and visitors.
> They whistled: This is *it*!
>
> Golden, whilst your frozen daiquiris
> whir at midnight, gleams on you his fur
> & silky & black.
> Mission accomplished, pal.

The War between Eros, Marriage, and the Family in
For Lizzie and Harriet

In 1973 Robert Lowell published three books. One of these, *History,* is a compendium of his musings on the public realm: states, battles, historical characters, the fortunes of nations and empires. The other two, *The Dolphin* and *For Lizzie and Harriet,* concern themselves with the poet's ruling preoccupation from *Life Studies* on: eros, marriage, and the family. These three books represent the flowering—or the metastasis—of *Notebook 1967–68,* the project he took on after the publication of *For the Union Dead* in 1964 and *Near the Ocean* in 1967.

Life Studies (1959) had popularized Confessional poetry, or—a better description, "the poetry of personal extremity"—bringing it to the attention of a larger reading public than is generally aware of poetry in the United States. The title poem of *For the Union Dead* was a public ode, an anthem of the Civil Rights movement for that segment of the population that reads the *New York Review of Books. Near the Ocean,* too, with the rhyming couplets of its title sequence, had a public, imperial grandeur.

In the political arena, Lowell had the knack of bringing to bear his influence as the most visible poet of his day. This he had done during the March on Washington in 1967, which helped to marshal public opposition to the Vietnam War—though he self-deprecatingly downplayed the sense of personal heroism that many involved in the antiwar movement attributed to themselves:

> Where two or three were flung together, or fifty,
> mostly white-haired, or bald, or women . . . sadly
> unfit to follow their dream, I sat in the sunset
> shade of our Bastille, the Pentagon,
> nursing leg- and arch-cramps, my cowardly,
> foolhardy heart; and heard, alas, more speeches,
> though the words took heart now to show how weak
> we were, and right

Within the context of the antiwar movement, his rhetoric here was deflationary. *Notebook* was galvanized by its author's sense of being the poetic diarist of his time, as well as the informed conscience of the movement. As evidenced by the list of dates at the back of the book, a lot was going on: Lowell's list begins with "The Vietnam War, 1967" and ends with "The Vietnam War, 1968." In between fall the Six Day Arab-Israeli War, the Riots in American cities, Che Guevara's death, the March on the Pentagon, the presidential campaigns of Eugene McCarthy and Robert Kennedy, the assassinations of Martin Luther King and Robert Kennedy, *les événements de Mai* in Paris, the 1968 Democratic Convention in Chicago, and so on.

Throughout his career, at least until the last few years of his life, when he seems to have lost it, Lowell had an uncanny sense of timing. Stanley Kunitz was impressed by his friend's rapt attention to the literary climate: "he watched its weather with the diligent attention of a meteorologist, studying its prevailing winds, regularly charting its high and low pressure area." His sense of the larger national mood was equally acute, and the original impulse for the *Notebook* was brilliantly simple. He would keep a poetic notebook. What went into it would be determined by what happened during the course of a year. It would be a sequence organized into fourteen-line units, which would not, unlike the lines of a sonnet, usually rhyme. Sometimes the line would be iambic pentameter, sometimes not.

> Notebook 1967–68: as my title intends, the poems in this book
> are written as one poem, jagged in pattern, but not a conglom-
> eration or sequence of related material. It is not a chronicle
> or almanac; many events turn up, many others of equal or

greater reality do not. This is not my diary, my confession, not a puritan's too literal pornographic honesty, glad to share private embarrassment, and triumph. The time is a summer, an autumn, a winter, a spring, another summer; here the poem ends, except for turned-back bits of fall and winter 1968. I have flashbacks to what I remember, and notes on old history. My plot rolls with the seasons. The separate poems and sections are opportunistic and inspired by impulse. Accident threw up subjects, and the plot swallowed them—famished for human chances.

So far, so good. Then, it seems to me, Lowell became lulled by the security of the form. The fourteen-liners became too easy to write. Lowell's friend and most reliable critic, Randall Jarrell—who died, significantly, in 1965, a year after *For the Union Dead*—had seen in his friend's early poetry a struggle between two forces. On the one hand there was "the Kingdom of Necessity":

> Into this realm of necessity the poems push everything that is closed, turned inward, incestuous, that blinds or binds. . . . But struggling within this like leaven, falling to it like light, is everything that is free or open, that grows or is willing to change: here is the generosity or openness or willingness that is itself salvation; here is "accessibility to experience"; this is the realm of freedom.

The "unrhymed sonnet" form hardened into "the kingdom of necessity." Lowell's daughter, Harriet, was not far off the mark when in one of these she commented, "You've got to call your *Notebook, Book of the Century,* / but it will take you a century to write, / then I will have to revise it, when you die." Revision, which was probably the most important thing Lowell taught his students, changed, when indulged in too long, into a vice. That language eventually came to seem an abstract medium cut off from human emotions is suggested by Jonathan Raban's comment in Hamilton's biography that Lowell's revisions became:

> a kind of gaming with words, treating them like billiard balls. For almost every sentence that Cal ever wrote if he thought it

made a better line he'd have put in a "never" or a "not" at the essential point. His favorite method of revision was simply to introduce a negative into a line, which absolutely reversed its meaning but very often would improve it. So that his poem on Flaubert ended with Flaubert dying, and in the first draft it went "Till the mania for phrases dried his heart"—a quotation from Flaubert's mother. Then Cal saw another possibility and it came out: "Till the mania for phrases enlarged his heart." It made perfectly good sense either way round, but the one did happen to mean the opposite of the other.

Elizabeth Bishop, memorializing her friend in "North Haven" the year before her own death, thought of nature's easy and unforced patterns of recurrence:

> The Goldfinches are back, or others like them,
> and the White-throated Sparrow's five-note song,
> pleading and pleading, brings tears to the eyes.
> Nature repeats herself, or almost does:
> *repeat, repeat, repeat; revise, revise, revise.*

The half-rhyme "does" repeats the rhyme of "eyes," or as the words assert, it *almost* does, with the full rhyme returning on "revise." In an Afterword to *Becoming a Poet,* David Kalstone's book about Bishop, Lowell, and Moore, James Merrill comments that in this poem, Bishop "finds in nature a poignant and oddly appropriate image, whereby his lifelong recyclings of earlier work come to seem not so much tortured as instinctive, part of a serene Arcadian world." This is a more benign interpretation than the one I have been arguing.

It is instructive but perhaps unfair to compare Lowell with Bishop, the two finest American poets of our immediate period (or is one engaging in Lowell's mania for ranking when one makes that sort of assessment?). Lowell had a breadth and resonance that Bishop never approached. She on the other hand had a natural grace and lightness of touch that Lowell marveled at. If for Bishop, orphaned by the age of six, life was often a grim struggle against loneliness, illness, and drink, she achieved in her work a kind of serenity for which everyone who loves her poems has reason to be grateful. In his sonnet period Lowell lost the sense of change and variety that is one of the joys of reading Bishop's poetry. Rather than move on to something fresh—which he had often accomplished in the earlier phases of his poetry—Lowell, at least in Bishop's eyes, was stuck repeating himself.

For this poet, whose lifeblood was change, to be alive was to revise. It was a knack he had learned from his early mentor, Allen Tate, who taught that a poem "must be tinkered with and recast until one's eyes pop out of one's head." Now his mania for change started to focus too narrowly on the material at hand. Instead of doing what he had done so often before, the craftsman in him bent like a jeweler over poems he had already written and tinkered with them—often to only minimal effect—rather than making the bold change that would have sprung him into a dramatically new style. Change would not come until *Day by Day*—and there only in part—published in 1977.

During the 1970s Bishop, who was six years older than Lowell, was bothered by her friend's way of picturing himself as older than he really was:

> I am now going to be very impertinent and aggressive. Please, *please* don't talk about old age so much, my dear old friend! You are giving me the creeps. . . . I don't feel much different than I did at 35—and I certainly am a great deal happier, most of the time. . . . I just *won't* feel ancient—I wish Auden hadn't gone on about it so his last years, and I hope you won't.

Yet Lowell, at fifty, wrote as if he were seventy, and sounded very much the valetudinarian:

> Dear Heart's-Ease,
> we rest from all discussion, drinking, smoking,
> pills for high blood, three pairs of glasses—soaking
> in the sweat of our hard-earned supremacy,
> offering a child our leathery love. We're fifty,
> and free! Young, tottering on the dizzying brink
> of discretion once, you wanted nothing,
> but to be old, do nothing, type and think.

Both of his parents had died in early middle age (he himself was to die at sixty). In his poem "Mother and Father 1" from *History*, "They say, 'I had my life when I was young.'" It's almost as though he were in a hurry to get old, as though he couldn't wait to die. In "Commander Lowell" from *Life Studies* he had even "cringed because Mother, new / caps on all her teeth, was born anew / at forty." The virtual readiness to die seems to have been shared, at least in this poem, by Lowell's father: "With seamanlike celerity, / Father left the Navy, / and deeded Mother his property." At the time of his own death, "he was resigned to dying," his friend William Alfred has said. "He knew he was going to die." His biographer Ian Hamilton has this to say: "Caroline Blackwood calls his death a 'suicide of wish': there were 'various things he said' at Castletown [the Irish country house where he and she had a flat] during his last week which made her think that he did not expect to live."

In the sequence "Mexico" from *For Lizzie and Harriet*, the poet depicts himself as "fifty, humbled with the years' gold garbage, / dead laurel grizzling my back like spines of hay"—a repellent image informed by a certain amount of self-disgust, and perhaps disingenuous as well, since honors were important to him. The description occurs during a sequence that tells of his affair with a younger woman: "you, some sweet, uncertain age, say twenty-seven, / untempted, unseared by honors or deception."

This affair is one of two that are alluded to in *For Lizzie and Harriet*. Poems about the two affairs are the subject of twenty-three of the sixty-seven poems in the book. One doesn't have to be a puritan to ask whether, since a third of the text concerns extramarital affairs, there isn't something inappropriate about the dedication to the poet's wife and daughter. Even someone who loves Lowell's poetry as much as I do has a hard time avoiding what on one level are simply questions of basic decency. Elizabeth Bishop's plain words about Lowell's use of his wife's letters keep coming to mind: *"art just isn't worth that much."*

It is not as though Lowell was unaware of the problem. Perhaps what other people might see as decency, he saw as hypocrisy. Morally, aesthetically, he maintained a stubborn loyalty to the fallen, the less-than-ideal, the humanly corrupted. This was a kind of self-assertion on the part of a man who at every stage of his life was made to believe he was in various ways unworthy. Having earlier described the summer rain in "Eye and Tooth" as "a simmer of rot and renewal," he rhymes it with "Even new life is fuel." He cherished the untidy life process. "Life is too short," he asserts in a poem to Elizabeth Hardwick, "to silver over this tarnish."

Surely Lowell was blinded, as everyone is at one time or another, by love. This facet of his personality has been written about but often misrepresented. In her 1991 biography of Anne Sexton, for instance, Diane Wood Middlebrook writes:

> The ambiguity about the status of women in Lowell's class [at Boston University] was enhanced by his reputation as a skirt-chaser. As one of his friends put it, "Cal had to be 'in love.' Poets were always in love." . . . There was always "a girl" somewhere in the background of his professional life, and during the manic phases of his mood swings, she was very much in the foreground. Lowell did not cultivate privacy in regard to his erotic adventures.

Perhaps Lowell's scorn of privacy partially answers the question I have raised about his including the poems about his affairs in a book dedicated to his wife and daughter. Perhaps he should be complimented for not being a hypocrite. It is undeniable that, as Anthony Hecht puts it in his memoir, "*Le Byron de Nos Jours,*" "Lowell's manic cycles almost always involved episodes of sexual adventurism." But I wonder whether this qualifies him as a "skirt-chaser." He was as much the pursued as the pursuer. Hecht sees him as a Byronic figure, and the analogy is more convincing than would on the surface appear plausible:

> The Byron comparison, while not to be pursued with Euclidean precision . . . is a fair one in some respects. Both poets were public figures and involved in the political events of their time; both were capable of devastating expressions of scorn for their opponents; both were powerful and handsome men; both were crippled, each in his own way; both were astonish-

ingly attractive to women; both were aristocrats by inheritance (somewhat shabby aristocrats) and democrats by generous instinct; both were the subject of scandalous gossip during and after their lifetime. . . . It may be added that both were bedeviled by a strict and relentlessly Puritan conscience, and Calvinistic anguish.

It is impossible, perhaps, to be fully sensitive or fully sympathetic to just how anguished Lowell was much of the time, despite the references to his troubled state of mind in poem after poem. "I hear / my ill-spirit sob in each blood cell, / as if my hand were at its throat" from "Skunk Hour" is one of the more familiar of these. Eros was one release, and perhaps the main release, from his pain. At some point most readers will tire of Lowell's "turmoil," but certainly the pathos of his great need will not be lost on the reader.

At the same time, one sympathizes with the objects—the victims, almost—of his manic "love": "Poor Child, you were kissed so much you thought you were walked on; / yet you wait in my doorway with bluebells in your hair." What Lowell calls "love" in these pages is another name for obsession: "When you left, I thought of you each hour of the day, / each minute of the hour, each second of the minute." When he looks back on this affair in the poem "Eight Months Later," his retrospective awareness acknowledges the link between his mania and the obsessiveness of love: "did anyone ever sleep with anyone / without thinking a split second he was God?"

Lowell's God strode right out of the Old Testament. In "The Quaker Graveyard in Nantucket" he wrote: "The Lord survives the rainbow of His will," which I take to mean that the Lord remains under no contractual obligation not to end the world by flood—as He promised Noah—if He so chooses. Certainly there existed in Lowell's mind an identification between the lover, God, and the outlaw. In the "Mexico" series the affair is described in these terms:

> Our conversation moved from lust to love,
> asking only coolness, stillness, conversation—
> then days, days, days, days . . . how can I love you more,
> short of turning into a criminal?

A startling association of ideas! But to love was, for Lowell, to break the law, and love was a battle. The clearest expression of this is in "Law," from *For the Union Dead:*

> Under one law,
> or two,
> to lie unsleeping,
> still sleeping on the battlefield . . .

Probably the "one law" here encompasses a married couple, and the "two" an adulterous couple. The battlefield metaphor comes to light again in the "Charles Riber" sequence, Lowell's account of the other affair in *For Lizzie and Harriet:*

> We lie parallel,
> parallel to the river, parallel
> to six roads—unhappy and awake,
> awake and naked, like a line of Greeks,
> facing a second line of Greeks—like them,
> willing to enter the battle, and not come out . . .
> morning's breathing traffic . . . its unbroken snore.

The lovers are two armies; here, interestingly, they are two armies of the same nation. Elsewhere Lowell seems convinced as to the differences between the sexes. Two pages earlier, he ends "Through the Night" with: "we are two species, even from outside— / a net trapped in the arms of another net."

Turn now from poems about adultery to what claims to be the center of *For Lizzie and Harriet:* poems about marriage and family. Lowell can hardly be accused of sentimentalizing his marriage—"If I can't whistle in the dark," he begins in "Dear Sorrow I," "why whistle?" The marriage itself he identifies, somewhat chillingly, as the moment "when / the Graces noosed you with my hard gold ring." In "New Year's Eve" he delivers this ambiguous tribute:

> My Darling, prickly hedgehog of the hearth,
> chocolates, cherries, hairshirt, pinks and glass—
> when we joined in the sublime blindness of courtship,

loving lost all its vice with half its virtue.
Cards will never be dealt to us fairly again.

The chocolates and cherries are conventional appeasements. Lowell presumably intends to wear the hairshirt himself. One hopes the glass is not broken! And given his decided bias in favor of vice, I'm not sure any romance of his could have functioned without it. He is the master of the ambiguous remark, and it's hard to know precisely how to take the last line. At times the ambiguities are sharp and skillful, at times too pat, as when he asks, "Can I be forgiven the life-waste of my lifework? / Was the thing worth doing worth doing badly?" Working one's way through the subtleties gets a bit tiring sometimes.

If *For Lizzie and Harriet* is not so brilliant a book as *The Dolphin,* for me it's more attractive—saner and more humane. The difference between the drawings Frank Parker did for the two books is significant: For *The Dolphin* he drew a long-haired figure being drawn head first into a whirlpool. His drawing on the title page of *For Lizzie and Harriet* shows a broad, weather-beaten evergreen tree, with a few birds flying around its topmost branches. Lowell discovered during this period that he could and would write about *anything,* and the pleasure he took in run-of-the-mill domesticity can be very pleasing, as in one of his poems to Harriet:

> A repeating fly, blueback, thumbthick—so gross,
> it seems apocalyptic in our house—
> whams back and forth across the nursery bed
> manned by a madhouse of stuffed animals,
> not one a fighter. It is like a plane
> dusting apple orchards or Arabs on the screen—
> one of the mighty . . . one of the helpless.

The characterization of the stuffed animals—"not one a fighter"—is nicely humorous. Who else but Lowell would, even jokingly, expect them to want to fight? The cliché that identifies everything as political is for once true. Seeing the fly, he would think of Israeli jets strafing Arabs in the desert. And following the Holocaust, Israel's militarism gives pointedness to Lowell's formulation: "one of the mighty . . . one of the helpless." Helpless himself in his own vulnerability, he proves himself also one of the mighty, by killing the fly.

Contentment is eroded by tensions between man and wife: *"We never see him now, except at dinner,"* his daughter complains, *"then you quarrel, and he goes upstairs."* Lowell the epigrammatist comments in "The Human Condition," "our wars were simpler than our marriages." Still, family pleasures and affections come across unforced and convincing in this book: "Some fathers may have some consideration," Harriet is quoted as saying, with just a touch of her mother's irony, "but he is so wonderfully eccentric, / drinking buttermilk and wearing red socks." At times the fond father's attempts to bridge disparities like summer camp and American history snap under the strain. Observing the counselors and kids gathered waiting for the ferry to take them home, Lowell speculates, "The Acadians must have gathered in such arcs; / a Winslow, our cousin, shipped them from Nova Scotia— / no malice, merely pushing his line of work." It comes across like an unconscious parody of his early poems about family history.

On the other hand, "Words for Muffin, a Guinea-Pig," is triumphantly unlikely, and much funnier than one would have guessed Lowell could be in print. His obsession with history and his remaining, at the same moment, thoroughly enmeshed in things that happen around the house, combine brilliantly. Here is the poem in its entirety:

> Of late they leave the light on in my entry,
> so I won't scare, though I never scare in the dark;
> I bless this arrow that flies from wall to window . . .
> five years and a nightlight given me to breathe—
> Heidegger said spare time is ecstasy. . . .
> I am not scared, although my life was short;
> my sickly breathing sounded like dry leather.
> *Mrs. Muffin!* It clicks. I had my day.
> You'll paint me like Cromwell with all my warts:
> small mop with a tumor and eyes too popped for thought.
> I was a rhinoceros when jumped by my sons.
> I ate and bred, and then I only ate,
> my life zenithed in the Lyndon Johnson 'sixties . . .
> this short pound God threw on the scales, found wanting.

More than any other poem I can think of, this gets Lowell's broad and outrageous sense of humor onto the page. Writing on *the Mills of the Kavanaghs* in 1952, Randall Jarrell wrote, "You feel, 'Yes, Robert Lowell would act like this if he were a girl'; but whoever saw a girl like Robert Lowell?" Whoever saw a *guinea pig* like Robert Lowell? The mock-elevation of the first line: "Of late" sets the tone of high incongruity, and then "my entry." What guinea pig has an "entry"? And what other guinea pig quotes Heidegger? Or takes such pains to convince itself it is not afraid? Or is so full of self-importance about its name as to exclaim, "*Mrs. Muffin!* It clicks," or to complain to her biographer and compare herself to Cromwell?

Lowell and the wife he calls "Old campaigner" in an affectionate reprise of his preoccupation with the war between the sexes make it, just barely, to the end of the book. "We could have done much worse," he says. "I hope we did / a hundred thousand things much worse!" The marriage, as we shall learn in *The Dolphin,* is about to break, though in an ending no one could have plotted so well as life itself did: Lowell died in a taxi cab on his way back to Elizabeth Hardwick's apartment in New York four years after these two collections were published. *For Lizzie and Harriet* is a troubled, grizzled, and often exasperated tribute to a lasting marriage: "old cars, old money, old undebased pre-Lyndon / silver, no copper rubbing through . . . old wives; / I could live such a too long time with mine." That ironic, bothered "too long" is pure Lowell. It's all highly qualified, but nonetheless tender for all that:

> Before the final coming to rest, comes the rest
> of all transcendence in a mode of being, hushing
> all becoming. I'm for and with myself in my otherness,
> in the eternal return of earth's fairer children,
> the lily, the rose, the sun on brick at dusk,
> the loved, the lover, and their fear of life,
> their unconquered flux, insensate oneness, painful "It
>   was. . . ."
> After loving you so much, can I forget
> you for eternity, and have no other choice?

The Dolphin
"Ransacking My Bags of Dust
for Silver Spoons"

Though *The Dolphin* won Robert Lowell a Pulitzer Prize in
1973—his second (the first was for *Lord Weary's Castle*)—the
poems in it turned out to be his most controversial. Part of the
dispute surrounded the poems themselves, whose fourteen-
line, unrhymed "sonnet" form many readers found repetitive
and undifferentiated. More troubling was Lowell's practice of
versifying and including in his book personal letters from his
second wife, Elizabeth Hardwick. The dolphin figures in the
book as Lowell's muse. Muse as the woman, Caroline Black-
wood, who became his third wife, to whom many of the poems
are addressed. And muse as the principle of delightful and
often dangerous novelty that Lowell held dear throughout his
life as a poet: "Any clear thing that blinds us with surprise, /
your wandering silences and bright trouvailles, / dolphin let
loose to catch the flashing fish." This poem, "Fishnet," the
first in the book, while darkened by some hard-won self-
knowledge, announces Lowell's *ars poetica* and affirms his
sense of the work he has done. The love story told in this book
is not a happy one; clearly Lowell was blinded by the surprise
of an infatuation that turned out to be perilous, and in certain
real ways, fatal.

The man who wrote "O to break loose. All life's grandeur /
Is something with a girl in summer" thrived on the exhilara-
tion of falling in love. Each new infatuation carried with it the
illusion that a new life might open up for him. His romantic
life was perfectly consistent with his life as an artist: he re-

invented his style and self over and over again in the same way that he kept falling in love. The idea of surprise as something that "blinds us" recurs later in the book, as the dolphin metamorphoses into a mermaid, the creature who lures men underwater to their deaths:

> Mermaid, why are you another species?
> "Because, you, I, everyone is unique."
> Does anyone ever make you do anything?
> "Do this, do that, do nothing; you're not chained.
> I am a woman or I am a dolphin,
> the only animal man really loves,
> I spout the smarting waters of joy in your face—
> rough weather fish, who cuts your nets and chains."
>
> "Mermaid Emerging"

One would be forcing a point to argue from this passage that Lowell regarded woman as "another species," since the mermaid is not only a particular permutation of woman's role but a particular woman. His sense of women's otherness is a question I will return to. First look at the last four lines of the poem:

> Yet my heart rises, I know I've gladdened a lifetime
> knotting, undoing a fishnet of tarred rope;
> the net will hang on the wall when the fish are eaten,
> nailed like illegible bronze on the futureless future.

The fishnet is poetry—the craft, the skill, the complex training that fits syntax, meter, diction, pacing, modulation, and so on to emotion, that coordinates mind and impulse. Surprisingly, Lowell sees the finished product as an empty net: the poem is what remains when the human elements of the drama have resolved themselves.

Lowell took immense pleasure in the act of writing. While many writers will say that they like *to have written* something but don't enjoy the writing itself, Lowell found the process actively sustaining. Paradoxically the pleasure, the release he found in writing, may be part of the problem in these poems. They may suffer from having been too much a form of escape for him. In a letter to Frank Bidart on September 4, 1976, he wrote:

> It's miraculous, as you told me about yourself, how often writing takes the ache away, takes time away. You start in the morning, and look up to see the windows darkening. I'm sure anything done steadily, obsessively, eyes closed to everything besides the page, the spot of garden . . . makes returning a jolt. The world you've been saved from grasps you roughly. Even sleep and dreams do this. I have no answer. I think the ambition of art, the feeding on one's soul, memory, mind etc., gives a mixture of glory and exhaustion.

The last four lines from "Fishnet" illustrate his tendency in the fourteen-line poems that make up *Notebook* and the three books it turned into—*The Dolphin, For Lizzie and Harriet,* and *History*—to lapse into an unsatisfying rhetoric where paradox becomes the favored trope. The fishnet, the poem, is "nailed like illegible bronze on the futureless future." Doesn't "illegible" need explaining? And why is the future "futureless"? Admittedly, the notion that we faced extermination was more convincing during the Cold War than it is now, but it sounds facile except when applied to the individual life. It is one example among many of the kind of statement that works equally well as either assertion or negation—an odd but very characteristic feature of Lowell's "sonnets." "Caligula" from *For the Union Dead* ends: "yours the lawlessness / of something simple that has lost its law, / my namesake, and the last Caligula." "Caligula 2," from *Notebook* and reprinted in *History*, ends: "yours the lawlessness / of something simple that has lost its law, / my namesake, not the last Caligula." The earlier version dissociates him from his namesake, the later version restores the identification. But how gripping is a reader likely to find the distinction?

The troubling symptom here is an impenetrable self-absorption. The dilemma of the "confessional" poet is how to make his own story compelling enough to keep the reader's attention. Lowell addressed the problem as early as "Eye and Tooth" from *For the Union Dead:* "I am tired. Everyone's tired of my turmoil." His dilemma, though, continued to be that his life was ultimately his only subject. When he writes in "Symptoms," "I soak, / examining and then examining / what I really have against myself," readers may have trouble staying interested in what was Lowell's main subject for at least fifteen years—a troubled, autobiographical subject matter that eventually came to seem overworked. Consider Frank O'Hara's reaction, quoted in Brad Gooch's biography, *City Poet,* to "Skunk Hour" from *Life Studies:*

> Lowell has . . . a confessional manner which [lets him] get away with things that are really just plain bad but you're supposed to be interested because he's supposed to be so upset. . . . I don't think that anyone has to get themselves to go and watch lovers in a parking lot necking in order to write a poem, and I don't see why it's admirable if they feel guilty about it. They should feel guilty.

About the pain in "Skunk Hour" O'Hara is being deliberately obtuse and insensitive. There's no doubt that Lowell was genuinely "upset." Too, O'Hara himself was determined, at all costs and for his own reasons, to put a cheerful face on things. But his criticism accurately registers an impatience one can easily feel about Lowell's self-flagellation.

Often, reading the fourteen-liners, one sympathizes with Lowell's straw man, "the reviewer sent by God to humble me / ransacking my bags of dust for silver spoons." A complex point is suggested if the lines, as they seem to, allude to the story of Joseph in exile in Egypt, who planted a silver cup in his brothers' bags of wheat so that it would be discovered as they left the country as a pretext for bringing them back to live with him in prosperity. These poems, if they fail in their larger ambitions, are nevertheless valuable for being a repository for Lowell's "silver spoons" (the metaphor, incidentally, linking his art with his aristocratic birth)—some of the best single lines ever written. For example, "but soon Victoria's manly oak was quartered, / knickknacks dropped like spiders from the whatnot" is like an exemplum from Pope's "Art of Poetry," demonstrating what can be accomplished by word sounds, by making the verse go slow and then fast.

The first line is slow and stately, making full use of the heroic associations of "manly oak" and "quartered." The second, speedier line is comical, playing the rapid initial spondee of "knickknacks" off against the final spondee of "whatnot" in a mischievous way—one of Lowell's subversive little jokes. While he is playing to a strength here, dealing in the generational history he can be so adept at, the poem ultimately flops: "Last century's quantity brick has a sour redness / that time, I fear, does nothing to appease, / condemned by age, rebuilt by desolation." What reader really gives a damn about that "sour redness"? One finds oneself asking what the point is. The Popean antithetical last line drifts aimlessly: What does it mean to say that last century's brick is "rebuilt by desolation"? There's something pompous about many last lines in these poems: "Our senses want to please us, if we please them." The cadence here says that the line should be either witty or profound, but it is neither.

Nor is Lowell's verse free of self-indulgent puns: "Surely good writers write all possible wrong." There is also the breezy, too-pat epigrammatic formulation: "you are packaged to the grave with me, / where nothing's opened by the addressee . . ." Many of the poems contain the verbal equivalent of the doodle: "that silly swelled tree is a spook with a twig for a head," for instance, though the same poem also contains some rather good description: "The courtesans and lions / swim in Carpaccio's brewing tealeaf color." And the poem is full of pleasant little non sequiturs—"the cat nibbles little shoots foretelling rain"—that give a wonderful sense of the poet's mental processes.

For someone who has followed Lowell's poetry all the way through his career, the sense of his mind in action during his mad periods in this book is of great interest. In *Lord Weary's Castle*, the poet's madness expresses itself through derangement of language. *Life Studies*, which more openly takes madness as its subject, looks at mental illness from the standpoint of one who has been cured. In a poem from *The Dolphin* like "Double-Vision," mental derangement, complicated by the anti-psychotic drugs, is explicitly the subject:

I tie a second necktie over the first;
no one is always waiting at the door,
and fills the window . . . sometimes a Burmese cat,
or maybe my Daughter on the shell of my glasses.
I turn and see persons, my pajama top
loose-knotted on the long thin neck of a chair—
make yourself at home. The cat walks out—
or does it? The room has filled with double-shadows,
sedation doubles everything I see. . . .
You can't be here, and yet we try to talk;
somebody else is farcing in your face,
we haggle at cross-purposes an hour.
While we are talking, I am asking you,
"Where is Caroline?" and you *are* Caroline.

How precise that "somebody else is farcing your face" is! And the complex nature of hallucination—not simply visual, but emotionally colored in the most subtle and telling way—in "maybe my Daughter on the shell of my glasses."

The moral question raised by *The Dolphin* is, as I have said earlier, the impropriety, the indecency even, of publishing Elizabeth Hardwick's letters as poems. Most of Lowell's literary friends, including W. H. Auden and Elizabeth Bishop, spoke out against his intention to publish the letters, though Frank Bidart loyally supported Lowell, saying that "the only thing posterity will not forgive you is a bad book." Twenty years have now passed. We have become posterity. This is not a bad book. As flawed and problematic as it is, it still has a measure of greatness.

As early as *The Mills of the Kavanaghs* Lowell deliberately introduced characters into his poetry as a counter to his own solipsism. The characters in *Life Studies* are what bring the book to life. But Lowell's use of the Hardwick material remains problematic. One doesn't have to have been involved personally to be appalled that he could let himself quote these lines:

["]That new creature,
when I hear her name, I have to laugh.

You left two houses and two thousand books,
a workbarn by the ocean, and two slaves
to kneel and wait upon you hand and foot—
tell us why in the name of Jesus." Why
am I clinging here so foolishly alone?

This is purely and simply indecent. That the man's wife presents herself and her daughter, even hyperbolically and ironically, as "two slaves"—isn't there at least a touch of braggadocio accompanying his publication of this? The question he asks himself, "Why / am I clinging here so foolishly alone?," lacks for me the urgency of the appeal contained in the letter he has just quoted. He has a perfect right to expose his own anguish, but what gives him the right to expose hers as well? Defenders of the book have cited "Dolphin," the last poem, with Lowell's assertion, "I have . . . / plotted perhaps too freely with my life, / not avoiding injury to others, / not avoiding injury to myself," as evidence that he took full responsibility for his actions: "my eyes have seen what my hand did." Adrienne Rich's assessment, which I quoted at greater length earlier, is to the point: "it is presumptuous to balance injury done to others with injury done to myself."

The book is cruel but not shallow. Its moral callousness may in fact be part of what gives it access to the raw emotional insights it attains. And it has to stand or fall on how compelling these insights are to the individual reader. Lowell probes a disturbing aspect of his own sexuality: his attraction to what he sees as the threatening, man-destroying female. As she changes in the poet's mind from lover to destroyer, she metamorphoses from dolphin to mermaid. The mermaid is traditionally pictured holding a mirror, which signifies her narcissism. For the danger of his attraction to the dolphin/mermaid who declares, "I spout the smarting waters of joy in your face— / rough weather fish, who cuts your nets and chains," Lowell has abandoned the less thrilling but more sustaining world of "Old wives and husbands," in "The Flaw," whose "gravestones wait / in couples with the names and half the date."

It's too bad that we see so little of the beginning of Lowell's infatuation with "the Dolphin"; the book records a love affair on the skids, and the lover's depictions of the beloved are far from flattering:

> I see you as a baby killer whale,
> free to walk the seven seas for game,
> warm-hearted with an undercoat of ice,
> a nerve-wrung back . . . all muscle, youth, intention,
> and skill expended on a lunge or puncture—

Clearly she is "deadlier than the male," the man-destroying female, the castrator out of psycho-sexual myth. One can even think of her as a slangy version of Robert Graves's White Goddess, the poet's muse and ultimately his nemesis: "She kills more bottles than the ocean sinks, / and serves her winded lovers' bones in brine, / nibbled at recess in the marathon."

This same figure has appeared in Lowell's poems before. She is the Gorgon, whose coiled snake hair Freud would see as phallic symbols, just as he would see the Gorgon's threat as the disguised threat of castration. In "Florence" of *For the Union Dead*, she is one of Lowell's monsters, whose cause he pleads: "Pity the monsters!" He distrusts the impulse of the monster-killing zealot: David who slays Goliath, Judith who cuts Holofernes' throat in the erotic privacy of his tent, Perseus who decapitates the Gorgon:

> My heart bleeds black blood for the monster.
> I have seen the Gorgon.
> The erotic terror
> of her helpless, big bosomed body
> lay like slop.
> Wall-eyed, staring the despot to stone,
> her severed head swung
> like a lantern in the victor's hand.

As a "monster" himself, alienated from society by his mental illness, Lowell distrusts the revolutionary zeal of the victorious hero. As someone who posits the sexually attractive woman as a destroyer of his masculinity, he has every reason to distrust the pairing of tyrant (especially if she is female) and tyrannicide.

Alan Williamson has made this crucial conflict the center of his penetrating study, *Pity the Monsters: the Political Vision of Robert Lowell.* In "Near the Ocean," in what Williamson calls a "free-floating, dreamlike scene," Lowell presents what could only very ironically be called a love story. The opening act, seemingly set within a theatre—"The house is filled"—dramatizes an act of tyrannicide: "The hero stands, / stunned by the applauding hands, / and lifts her head to please the mob . . ." By a rapid shift, the victim is revealed to be the mother: "And if she's killed // his treadmill heart will never rest— / his wet mouth pressed to some slack breast." He becomes a figure whose neurosis is well glossed in a book that enjoyed wide currency in the late 1960s, *Life Against Death,* by Norman O. Brown: "In man, the neurotic animal, the instinctual compulsion to repeat turns into its opposite, the quest for novelty, and the unconscious aim of the quest for novelty is repetition."

Having neatly dramatized the repetitive neurosis, the poem supplies some perspective by referring to earlier civilizations, where

> Older seas
> and deserts give asylum, peace
> to each abortion and mistake.
> Lost in the Near Eastern dreck,
> the tyrant and tyrannicide
> lie like the bridegroom and the bride

Lowell never quite specifies who "they"—the lovers in "Near the Ocean"—are, but we see them in the sordid setting of "some subway-green coldwater flat," living in "high delirious squalor, food / burned down with vodka . . . menstrual blood / caking the covers." Later, after an estrangement, they meet again, "dead sober, cured, recovered," living a life containing no "ocean," no joy—not even the pain-tinged joy of their earlier meetings. The sense is that there would be no point in living without the primal sexual force of everything that is represented by the ocean: "sand, / Atlantic ocean, condoms, sand." Since there is no choice, no way out, Lowell in this poem dedicated to E. H. L.—Elizabeth Hardwick Lowell—makes the existential commitment:

> A hand, your hand then! I'm afraid
> to touch the crisp hair on your head—
> Monster loved for what you are,
> till time, that buries us, lay bare.

The "crisp" hair seems pubic, reminiscent of the snaky hair of the Gorgon or Medusa.

The notion of facing the Gorgon clearly resonated for Lowell, because after having aired the scene in "Florence" and "Near the Ocean," he brings it up again in "Pointing the Horns of the Dilemma" from *The Dolphin:*

> From the dismay of my old world to the blank
> new—water-torture of vacillation!
> The true snakepit isn't monodrama Medea,
> the gorgon arousing the serpents in her hair;
> it's a room to walk with no one else, to walk,
> take thought, unthink the thought and listen for nothing

These thoughts occur at the point in the story where Lowell starts seriously regretting the choice he has made: "I draw a card I wished to leave unchosen, / and discard the one card I had sworn to hold." Drama becomes melodrama—we start to wonder whether our attention can be held by the spectacle of a middle-aged man trying to decide whether to leave his new wife for his old. It's hardly the stuff of high drama: "one man, two women, the common novel plot." What makes this triangle even less glamorous is that conflict over children is one of the main bones of contention. In "Pointing the Horns of the Dilemma," an accusatory voice, presumably Caroline's, says *"your real sickness is a fretful / deafness to little children."*

It's always fruitful to see modern poets like Pound and Eliot against the background of Victorian poetry, which they were much more familiar with than we are. Lowell's favored precursor among the Victorians was Arnold, but here one feels that George Meredith's sonnet sequence *Modern Love* holds interesting parallels. In both *The Dolphin* and *For Lizzie and Harriet* we find ourselves, surprisingly, in the modern world of remarried couples with combined families. Lowell's subject, certainly from *Life Studies* on, is the family—its stresses, its pathology, but also its nurturing qualities.

As is always the case with Lowell, one is aware of how the world on the page and the real world interface. In a recent issue of *Vanity Fair* there was a feature story on Caroline Blackwood's daughter Ivana, who had taken Lowell as her surname and was working as a model in New York. Caroline's neglectful attitude toward children—both as alluded to in *Vanity Fair* and as it filters through Lowell's poems—would shock most middle-class parents. The conflict of values is, to an extent, right out of Henry James, where relatively provincial and relatively puritanical Americans (often from Boston) encounter European sophistication:

> "My cousin really learned to loathe babies,
> she loved to lick the palate of her Peke,
> as if her tongue were trying a liqueur—
> what I say should go into your *Notebook*. . . .
> I'd rather dose children on morphine than the churches."

I had taken this dramatic monologue to be an acerbic portrait of Blackwood herself—the attitude is not inconsistent with other poems Lowell wrote on the subject—until I came upon an interview with her in the September 1993 *Town and Country:*

Did Robert Lowell ever have the experience of meeting your mother?

Yes, and then he wrote some lines to express his horror of her: "She loved to lick the palate of her Peke, / as if her tongue were trying a liqueur . . ." You see, she always has a Peke; she has, you might say, a permanent Peke. In fairness to Cal, he was doing not only my mother but a portrait of a person like that—of a society woman endlessly licking the palate of her Pekingese and just being awful to her children.

Against this kind of attitude toward children is set the humorous, commonsensical tone of Elizabeth Hardwick's letters:

"You insist on treating Harriet as if she / were thirty or a wrestler—she is only thirteen. / She is normal and good because she had normal and good / parents." One man, two women, and the children of all three. Hardwick comes to life through her letters, with their affection, their passion, and with their occasional note of friendly sarcasm:

> ["]I long to see
> your face and hear your voice, and take your hand—
> I'm watching a scruffy, seal-colored woodchuck graze
> on weeds, then lift his greedy snout and listen;
> then back to speedy feeding. He weighs a ton,
> and has your familiar human aspect munching."

With two characters as superbly drawn as Blackwood and Hardwick, perhaps one was hasty in condemning Lowell's use of quotations on moral grounds. An unexpected result of the way the two women dominate the story is that Lowell himself tends to disappear: "I come on walking off-stage backwards," as he puts it at one point. A poem that makes his tangentiality to the lives of the two women explicit is "The Couple," in which Caroline dreams she is walking and talking with Elizabeth:

> ["]Our conversation had a simple plot,
> a story of a woman and a man
> versifying her tragedy—
> we were talking like sisters . . . you did not exist."

"The Wristwatch Is Taken
from the Wrist"

To read Robert Lowell's last book, *Day by Day*, published shortly before his death in 1977, is to accompany the poet on a valedictory retrospective of his life and work. This is the most elegiac of his books. In poem after poem he says good-bye not only to old friends but to old ideas—the ruling ideas of his time. He continues to feel ambivalent about the third of his troubled marriages. Ambivalence was Lowell's characteristic stance—a stance that positioned him ideally to embody many of the conflicts of his period. When he died in a taxicab on the way to Elizabeth Hardwick's apartment in Manhattan after a flight from London, he was carrying, wrapped in brown paper, the famous portrait of Caroline Blackwood, *Girl in Bed*, painted by her first husband, Lucian Freud. In an interview in the September 1993 issue of *Town and Country*, Blackwood says that attendants at the hospital had to break Lowell's arms to remove the picture from his grasp.

Day by Day has the overall effect of an almost posthumous work: On the last page of Ian Hamilton's biography of Lowell, William Empson's words on *King Lear* are invoked:

> The scapegoat who has collected all this wisdom for us is viewed at the end with a sort of hushed envy, not I think really because he has become wise but because the general human desire for experience has been so glutted in him; he has been through everything.

> We that are young
> Shall never see so much, nor live so long.

The use of the verb "see" illuminates this unusually visual poet's experience. In the last section of the book he attempts to enunciate a visually based aesthetic that is only partially substantiated in his practice. As to the length of his life: in terms of an ordinary human lifetime, Lowell was not really old. But he filled his consignment of years with more involvement, personal and public, than most people manage to do. Elizabeth Bishop's chiding of Lowell for what she saw as a premature embrace of old age looks, from the vantage point of his relatively early death, unprescient. Both friends had much less time than Bishop, the older of the two, could guess. She herself would die in 1979. Lowell's premonition that his own life span would be cut off early, as his parents' had been, turns out to have been uncannily accurate.

Far from engaging in the typical, unseemly denial of aging and death, Lowell was almost in a hurry to get old and even to die. In *For the Union Dead,* written before he had reached fifty, he was ready in "The Flaw" to elegize Elizabeth Hardwick and himself:

> Old wives and husbands! Look, their gravestones wait
> in couples with the names and half the date—
> one future and one freedom. In a flash,
> I see us whiten into skeletons,
> our eager, sharpened cries, a pair of stones,
> cutting like shark-fins through the boundless wash.

Perhaps, to an extent, Lowell even romanticizes their deaths. Ten years later, on the contrary, the grim details of a hard-to-diagnose illness rather than an idealized notion of death recommend themselves to the poet's attention in "Day by Day." A preternatural "seriousness," a brutal realism, have consistently been part of his arsenal, so his accuracy in rendering the symptoms of what look like foreshadowings of his fatal heart disease should not come as a surprise. In "Our Afterlife II," addressed to his old friend Peter Taylor, he chills us with his clarity:

> My thinking is talking to you—
> last night I fainted at dinner
> and came nearer to your sickness,

nearer to the angels in nausea.
The room turned upside-down,
I was my interrupted sentence,
a misdirection tumbled back alive
on a low, cooling black table.

Faced with the direst of eventualities, his directness, the accuracy of his words, are at the ready. The writer's image of himself as an interrupted sentence is a humorous and lovely figure. One might well imagine how his cousin Harriet Winslow, paralyzed, an invalid for years, must have appreciated "Soft Wood," his *For the Union Dead* poem to her, not only for its affectionate tone but for its unsentimentalized acknowledgment of her illness:

I think of you far off in Washington,
breathing in the heat wave
and air-conditioning, knowing
each drug that numbs alerts another nerve to pain.

In "Endings"—one of the many poetic farewells to family members and friends which give *Day by Day* its elegiac tone—Lowell, older now, relates his own symptoms to hers:

You joked of your blackouts,
your abstractions,
comic and monumental
even for Washington.
You woke wondering why
you woke in another room,
you woke close to drowning.
Effects are without cause;
your doctors found nothing.
A month later you were paralyzed
and never unknotted . . .

Because, as "Epilogue," the last poem in the book puts it, "We are poor passing facts," we are "warned by that to give / each figure in the photograph / his living name." The accuracy of observation, the determination to do justice to fact—though it is highly questionable how faithful Lowell was to fact even when he thought he was—can in places give the realism of these poems a certain heroic air:

> A small spark tears at my head,
> a flirting of light brown specks in the sky,
> explosive pinpricks,
> an unaccountable lapse of time.

One's final response to *Day by Day* is likely to be complicated and hard to describe. Part of the complication is a certain awe when faced with the last work of a great artist. That this is the last work Lowell left, that there will never be a new Lowell poem to read, informs part of our response, prompting us to look back over the entire *oeuvre*.

These feelings of retrospective awe are complicated by a sense that many of the poems are off-puttingly oblique. Some of them read more like notes for poems than inspired utterances. The opening of "Phillips House Revisited," which finds Lowell hospitalized for a heart condition in the same place his grandfather died, sounds undeveloped, jotted down in haste: "Something sinister and comforting / in this return after forty years' arrears / to death and Phillips House." Many of these writings are willful. In some of them I simply don't understand the logic. And then there is the suspicion that often no sequential logic is intended. I am not speaking of the "difficulty" that good poems often achieve. Perhaps the most intriguing aspect of the book is that the poems' obliquity, their lack of interest in "making sense," is guided, at least ostensibly, by a consistent aesthetic. Interestingly, this aesthetic is announced only in the last few poems in the book. "Shifting Colors" ends with these lines:

> I am too weak to strain to remember, or give
> recollection the eye of a microscope. I see
> horse and meadow, duck and pond,
> universal consolatory
> description without significance,
> transcribed verbatim by my eye.

This is not the directness that catches
everything on the run and then expires—
I would write only in response to the gods,
like Mallarmé who had the good fortune
to find a style that made writing impossible.

Renunciation of memory, "description without significance,"
then, consoles. But how, as the next stanza—a ready example
of the obliquity I mentioned above—challenges us to accept,
does this brand of description differ from "the directness that
catches / everything on the run and then expires"? The next
line seems to say that Lowell would always prefer to write only
under the urging of inspiration—though too many of the
poems in this book read as if they were written just for the
sake of writing. This circumstance does not, one must quickly
add, exclude brilliant images, observations, and lines. If the
last two lines are not simply a joke not meant to be looked at
too closely, does Lowell think he would be happier giving up
poetry altogether? That strains credibility: this is a man whose
existence without his writing would be impossible to imagine.

Another poem, "Grass Fires," asserts baldly:

In the realistic memory
the memorable must be foregone;
it never matters,
except in front of our eyes.

If Lowell really believes that memorable events "must be fore-
gone," he would have to throw out most of what he had writ-
ten. On the other hand, a poet so wholeheartedly dedicated to
the new might relish the task. Still, Lowell's various statements
on observation, memory, and the imagination are just too con-
tradictory to form a consistent position. Is a poet required to
take a consistent position? No. But this is Lowell's most discur-
sive book; it markedly takes positions on poetics and thus asks
to be responded to intellectually.

Earlier, Lowell had been bothered that students of his po-
ems found it too easy to find "keys" to the work. "Maybe I
throw in too much Freud," he wrote me in 1969, "I try to use
him two thirds (?) skeptically and playfully. Even then [while

writing *Life Studies*] I found his Faith harder to take straight than the Pope's." Yet Lowell was in therapy with a Freudian analyst for several years preceding *Life Studies,* and I think he had absorbed more of Freud's point of view than he was aware.

As early as 1965, in the original version of "Waking Early Sunday Morning," which appeared in the *New York Review of Books,* Lowell was questioning the very notion of significance, of "great subjects," of meaningful symbols, in his poetry:

> I lie here on my bed apart,
> and when I look into my heart,
> I discover none of the great
> subjects: death, friendship, love and hate—
> only old china doorknobs, sad,
> slight, useless things to calm the mad.

The china doorknob held his attention in an almost obsessive way. Almost as soon as he had put the Freudianism of *Life Studies* behind him, he began trying to come to terms with the notion that whatever attracted his eye would become the true subject of his poetry. The eye becomes the arbiter of what he will write about, the eye tyrannizes him in a way, as is clear from the *For the Union Dead* poem, "Eye and Tooth": "No oil / for the eye, nothing to pour / on these waters or flames." Significantly, these lines are followed directly by his famous statement, "I am tired. Everyone's tired of my turmoil."

Again, in "Dolphin," the final poem in the book of the same name, Lowell evokes sight as a way of acknowledging action: "my eyes have seen what my hand did." The verb tenses, interestingly, have their own story to tell. Sight, for which the present perfect tense is employed, continues from then to now; action occurs in the past definite, and is final. Since Lowell's "Epilogue" to *Day by Day* is brief, and since it sums up his aesthetic of writing at the end of his life, I will quote it whole:

Epilogue

Those blessèd structures, plot and rhyme—
why are they no help to me now

> I want to make
> something imagined, not recalled?
> I hear the noise of my own voice:
> *The painter's vision is not a lens,*
> *it trembles to caress the light.*
> But sometimes everything I write
> with the threadbare art of my eye
> seems a snapshot,
> lurid, rapid, garish, grouped,
> heightened from life,
> yet paralyzed by fact.
> All's misalliance.
> Yet why not say what happened?
> Pray for the grace of accuracy
> Vermeer gave to the sun's illumination
> stealing like the tide across a map
> to his girl solid with yearning.
> We are poor passing facts,
> warned by that to give
> each figure in the photograph
> his living name.

This announced eschewal of plot and rhyme represents a renunciation of artificiality both in concept and in style. Lowell wrote often of plot in *The Dolphin,* most notoriously in the line, "one man, two women, the common novel plot." The same poem ends with words apparently quoted out of a letter from Elizabeth Hardwick: *"Don't you dare mail us the love your life denies; / do you really* know *what you have done?"* A good question; there is something heartless and dangerous about speaking of one's own life as though it were a novel.

The sense of "Epilogue" becomes problematic almost immediately when the author announces his allegiance not to memory but to the imagination. By arguing that the painter's vision "trembles to caress the light," Lowell gives realism an emotional coloration. Then he laments that his own realism—"paralyzed by fact"—too much resembles photography and not painting. It's hard to say exactly what he means by "All's misalliance." I think he means, consciously or not, that he can't make his ideas fit his practice. If, to paraphrase Yeats, we make rhetoric out of our quarrels with others and poetry out of our quarrels with ourselves, certainly this poem is a quarrel with the self. "Yet why not say what happened?" he asks with a sort of exasperated shrug. It is meant, one would think, to be a rhetorical question.

But one feels provoked to speak up and answer: if you just say what happened, then you lose the interest of readers who don't find your own life as urgently fascinating as you do. Lowell's reply in the last eight lines of the poem is that an inspired "accuracy" amounts to "grace." Because our mortality and the brevity of our lives is in itself so poignant, then memorialization—which takes up much of this book, as well as much of Lowell's whole *oeuvre*—is inherently valuable, this despite his having earlier declared in "Grass Fires," that "In the realistic memory / the memorable must be foregone."

An extreme example of poetry as just jotting down whatever comes to mind is "Wellesley Free." The poem wanders aimlessly from the leaf-blower operating outside, to a fleeting memory of the poet's school days, to a description of the room where he is sleeping. Then he tells us "I cannot read," and later that "I cannot sleep solo, / I loathe age with terror" and finally trails off: "70° outside, / and almost December." This poem should have been edited out of the collection.

The uncricical embrace of writing as process, which made the unrhymed "sonnets" seem to lose focus and almost turn their backs on their readers, became a serious problem for the poet from *Notebook* on. Daniel Hoffman, as friendly a reader as one can imagine, characterizes, in the *Gettysburg Review* in 1993, the *Notebook* period in these terms: "The yawning monster wouldn't stop—he soon revised and enlarged the book, republishing the new version as *Notebook,* and that also to be revised, enlarged, in an endless flood of unrhymed sonnets. By 1973 the machine had disgorged several hundred poems." One would hardly want to tar Robert Lowell with the brush of "poetry as therapy," but, oddly, he was not untouched by this confusion that has put serious art and basket weaving in the same category. He had even benefited from it: he started writing "91 Revere Street" as a prose memoir suggested by his psychiatrist. And *Life Studies* poems like "My Last Afternoon with Uncle Devereux Winslow" began as prose. At the end of "Unwanted," a critique of his tendency to see poetry as therapy, which I will look at in more detail later, Lowell asks an unanswerable and desperate question: "Is getting well ever an art, / or art a way to get well?"

The fusion of life and art that had been Lowell's genius from *Life Studies* on apparently blinded him to something essential that goes into a poem. Good poems have enough magnetism as objects or events to engage the reader. They stand on their own without reference to biography. Lowell more and more presumed his readers' knowledge of his life. He seems to have subsumed the act of writing so thoroughly into the personal realm that he lost the artist's edge. An indication that writing had become simply an activity rather than a means to the end of making poems with a life of their own, is suggested by Lowell's question to a doctor at the asylum where he was hospitalized in England:

> "These days of only poems and depression—
> what can I do with them?
> Will they help me to notice
> what I cannot bear to look at?"

If his poems are "only poems," if they are meant to help their author, one can hardly wonder why they lose their attraction for the reader. And then if the poet posits the supremacy of pure observation, one is much closer to understanding what is missing in Lowell's late poetry.

There are plenty of times when his confidence in his newly formulated philosophy of writing wavers. The poem that most closely resembles his *Life Studies* belief in psychological causality is "Unwanted."

> I read an article on a friend,
> as if recognizing my obituary:
> "Though his mother loved her son consumingly,
> she lacked a really affectionate nature;

so he always loved what he missed."
This was John Berryman's mother, not mine.

The way Lowell follows up on this psychological clue is reminiscent of the insistent self-analysis of his most Freudian period: "Often with unadulterated joy, / Mother, we bent by the fire / rehashing Father's character." Here it is the poet's own character getting rehashed. The difference now, though, is that Lowell analyzes his habit of self-absorbed analysis: "Alas, I can only tell my own story— / talking to myself, or reading, or writing, / or fearlessly holding back nothing from a friend."

What one can't help noticing, though, is how much of what Lowell was able to bring to *Life Studies* is missing even in the poems in this book that resemble those in the earlier book. The detailed panorama of social life, for instance—as though Lowell were an anthropologist of his own culture, noticing everything and rendering the feel of it with percepts and images, gossipy anecdotes, cameo appearances and pitch-perfect quotations from his characters. The question is not: "Yet why not say what happened?" The question is how finely, in what detail, with what humor, with how well-rendered a "surround" one says what happened.

Yet this is a meaty book, informed by an acute historical sense, full of moving retrospectives, reflections on aging, and poems to old friends. Lowell's world-weary tone is earned, as suggested by Empson's allusion to *King Lear*. No one is in a better position that Robert Lowell to chronicle the decline in the influence of Freud's ideas: "Dreams," he comments, "they've had their vogue, / so alike in their modernist invention." In "Since 1939" Lowell anticipates the end of Communism. The *frisson* of W. H. Auden's early work forms a backdrop for the poem's insights into a curious phenomenon of our times: the obsolescence of a political doctrine that promised the end of history, seen through the eyes of the generation who came of age in the immediate postwar period:

> We missed the declaration of war,
> we were on our honeymoon train west;

> we leafed through the revolutionary thirties'
> *Poems* of Auden, till our heads fell down
> swaying with the comfortable
> ungainly gait of obsolescence . . .

Having elsewhere defined history as that which we cannot see, Lowell labors to make visible the transition of ideas from revolutionary to outmoded: "I see another girl reading Auden's last book. / She must be very modern, / she dissects him in the past tense." His ironic use of the word "modern" here reinforces how difficult it is for our century, whose chief cultural movements all defined themselves under the banner of Modernism, to see itself as reentering that elusive continuum called history. Auden "is historical now as Munich, / and grew perhaps / to love the rot of capitalism." The poem brilliantly captures the confused sense of suspension experienced by those who have experienced and assented to the doctrines of Communism and Modernism: "In our unfinished revolutionary now, / everything seems to end and nothing to begin."

Though capable of the insight and economy of that formulation, Lowell, who has applied himself to the task of understanding history more assiduously than anyone since Pound, is clearly at a loss about where to go next. So he ruminates aimlessly:

> England like America has lasted
> long enough to fear its past,
> the habits squashed like wax,
> the gay, the prosperous,
> their acid of outrage . . .

His style fails him here. If one is going to generalize and make pronouncements, as the Augustan poets did, rhyme and meter can at least lend shapeliness and sonority to the enterprise. Lowell accomplished this in the rhyming stanza he used in *Near the Ocean:*

> No weekends for the gods now. Wars
> flicker, earth licks its open sores,
> fresh breakage, fresh promotions, chance

assassinations, no advance.
Only man thinning out his kind
sounds through the Sabbath noon, the blind
swipe of the pruner and his knife
busy about the tree of life . . .

Perhaps I have been too vigorous in pointing out the book's flaws. *Day by Day* contains some great elegiac moments, and these are its lasting achievement. "Our Afterlife I," the first of the two poems addressed to Peter Taylor, begins with an image of two Tennessee cardinals in migration—Taylor was a native Tennessean, and some of Lowell's apprentice days as a poet were spent in that Southern state. Following through on the image of the birds, the poem ends with a moment of pure elegiac transcendence:

We are things thrown in the air
alive in flight . . .
our rust the color of the chameleon.

He notes the "rust" of age and other natural processes, like the rain's "simmer of rot and renewal" and the "triangular blotch / of rot on the red roof" in an earlier poem, "Eye and Tooth." In a poem here about Milgate, Caroline Blackwood's ancestral manor house, Lowell characteristically celebrates decay and decline as few other poets do: "It is a natural life. Nettles / subdue the fugitive violet's bed, / a border of thistles hedges the drive." He is also capable of startlingly original images, such as New York as a cigarette lighter in "Death of a Critic":

Now the lifefluid goes
from the throwaway lighter,
its crimson, cylindrical, translucent
glow grows pale—

From a Brazilian *ex voto* sent to him by Elizabeth Bishop, a primitive head meant to be offered in church as a thanks-offering, Lowell spins "Thanks-Offering," a touching little poem expressing his relief at being himself again after one of his manic attacks: "Something has been taken off, / a wooden winter shadow— / goodbye nothing. I give thanks." Described, it comes alive:

>   especially
>   its shallow, chiseled ears,
>   crudely healed scars lumped out
>   to listen to itself, perhaps, not knowing
>   it was made to be given up.

With the wooden head as an emblem, Lowell deftly turns the object around to himself: "This winter, I thought / I was created to be given away."

That kind of directness and clarity were too often lacking in the three books that preceded *Day by Day*. Of the poet's last book, a sympathetic reader would like to agree with Louis Simpson that "we are back with the fascinating, superbly gifted poet of *Life Studies* and *For the Union Dead*." Simpson's statement perhaps embodied a wish more than a certainty. Certainly Lowell had turned a corner and was on the way back to finding himself as a poet, just as he was on the way back to his second wife, who had stood by him through it all, when he was struck down by a heart attack. As Peter Taylor wrote in his obituary on Lowell, he got the kind of death he always said he wanted: "a natural death, no teeth on the ground, no blood about the place." But he died before he had the chance to make one of those startling poetic metamorphoses he was capable of. Elizabeth Bishop wrote in her elegy on him,

>   You left North Haven, anchored in its rock,
>   afloat in mystic blue . . . And now—you've left
>   for good. You can't derange, or re-arrange,
>   your poems again. (But the Sparrows can their song.)
>   The words won't change again. Sad friend, you cannot
>   change.

UNDER DISCUSSION
Donald Hall, General Editor

Volumes in the Under Discussion series collect reviews and essays about individual poets. The series is concerned with contemporary American and English poets about whom the consensus has not yet been formed and the final vote has not been taken. Titles in the series include:

Please write for further information on available editions and current prices.

Ann Arbor   **The University of Michigan Press**